THE ENGLISH RUNES

Secrets of Magic, Spells and Divination

Suzanne Rance

Dragon House

First Printed 2017

Published by
Dragon House

Copyright © 2017 Suzanne Rance

Cover Art © 2017 Emma Martin

All rights reserved. No part of this publication may be reproduced, distributed, or transmitted in any form or by any means, including photocopying, recording, or other electronic or mechanical methods, without the prior written permission of the author, except in the case of personal use and certain other non-commercial uses permitted by copyright law. For permission request, email the author at the address below.

This book may not be lent, resold, hired out or otherwise disposed of by way of trade in any form of binding or cover other than that in which it is published, without prior consent.

suzanne@suzannerance.co.uk
www.suzannerance.co.uk

ISBN 978 0 9957264 0 6

For
Kevin, Charlotte, Gwynn and Kat

Acknowledgements

I would like to extend my grateful thanks to the following people without whom this book would not exist.

Deborah Westmancoat for kick starting this process with a challenge and for offering to proof read the result. A promise she has kept and undertaken whilst becoming an increasingly successful British Contemporary Artist.

Stephen Pollington for writing the foreword, permission to use his translation of the *Old English Rune Poem* and for checking my manuscript, Ic ðoncie ðé.

Emma Martin for her beautiful charcoal artwork that brings my book cover to life. A piece of art created from trees expressing the place of trees and nature in giving life to the English runes.

My copy editor Sarah Nisbet of Inkshed Editorial, whose knowledge of history and common sense approach ensures that I will have no hesitation in asking her again.

I would also like to thank Kevin Poole for his encouragement and support throughout, and Charlotte Rance for her wise counsel on all things pragmatic. Also to Heidi McNie, a big thank you for being there when I came up with new ideas, both good and bad, and for walking the land with me.

Last but by no means least my pagan and heathen friends for your unending encouragement.

Contents

Foreword 1

Introduction 3

Part 1   Runes and the English Runes 5

Runes and their history 7

    Old English runes and their relationship to the Elder Futhark 8

    The Old English Rune Poem manuscript 10

    The Old English Rune Poem and the life of the early English 13

Part 2   The Futhorc 17

Feoh – Wealth 19

Ur – Aurochs 22

Þorn – Thorn 25

Ōs – God 28

Rād – Riding 31

Cēn – Torch 34

Gyfu – Gift 37

Wen – Happiness 39

Hægl – Hail 42

Nyd – Need 45

Is – Ice 48

Gēr – Harvest 51

Ēoh – Yew 54

Peorð – Gaming 57

Eolhx – Elk 60

Sigel – Sun 63

Tīr – Tiw (a god) 66

Beorc – Birch 69

Eh – Horse 7
Man – Mankind 7
Lagu – Water (Large body of)..7
Ing – Ing (a god, thought to be Frea) 8
Ēðel – Homeland...8
Dæg – Day 8
Āc – Oak...9
Æsc – Ash 9
Yr – Bow of yew..9
Īar – Beaver...9
Ēar – Grave, one of the sea or the earth 10
Part 3   Wyrd 10
What is Wyrd? 10
    Using runes to influence Wyrd 11
Part 4   Making and working with runes 11
How to make your own runes 11
    What if I can't make my own runes? 11
How to work with your runes 12
Part 5   Divination 12
What is meant by divination 12
    Reading for yourself 12
    Reading for others 12
Part 6   Magical uses 13
    Magical formulae...13
    Bind runes and mirror runes 13
    How to make an amulet or talisman.................................13
Part 7   Galdor 13
What is Galdor? 14

Finding your voice 142
Singing the Runes into being 145
Appendix **147**
Rune table 147
Bibliography **153**
Companion Journals: 154

Foreword

In this slender volume, the reader in search of runic knowledge will find much to challenge and entertain. The esoteric and exoteric uses of the runes have been debated in academic and folklore circles for decades - indeed, centuries - so Suzanne Rance wisely offers no one-size-fits-all solutions to the puzzles associated with such knowledge and its transmission.

The strength of Suzanne's book is the emphasis on the Old English Rune Poem (arguably our only source of the rune-names drawn from a near-contemporary document) and one aspect of that work which is easily overlooked by the non-specialist reader. Each verse of the poem is self-contained and offers insight into the nature of the word which is the rune's name. But Old English verse is not a straightforward medium of expression, and multiple meanings are the norm rather than the exception. Ambiguity is indeed the hallmark of early Anglo-Saxon art in every branch - visual as well as verbal - and the subtleties of the language are not easily captured. All credit then to Suzanne for highlighting this often overlooked aspect of the tradition.

Careful study of the runes and working through the text of this book will reward the student who wishes to understand the rudiments of runic tradition.

Steve Pollington
Essex February, 2017

Introduction

You are probably familiar with Runes, an old European lettering system. They can be found widely in literature and film; however, these Runes are usually the Elder Futhark. What people are less aware of is that the English have their own Runes, steeped in the heritage of our ancient land. This book is designed to help you discover the runes found in *The Old English Rune Poem* and, through this, find out more about the lives of the early English and how they interacted with them. We will briefly look at their history and culture and explore their use in an attempt to breathe life into our ancient past.

I hope to persuade you to find a place in your hearts for the English runes. The British have been known to joke 'First there were the Romans and then it was dark for ages', but now things are changing. The post-Roman period may once have been known as the 'Dark Ages' but we can step out of this Victorian view; we can discover for ourselves how informed and surprisingly like us the early English people were, but living in a less technologically advanced world.

Over the years the study of runes has been split between those who are only interested in the academic, literary and historical aspects and those interested only in the esoteric aspect. This book attempts to close the gap a little by taking meaning and inspiration directly from the academic and applying it to the esoteric; trying to step in the shoes of the early English. Stephen Pollington is a historian and expert in Old English language and culture and his modern English translation has been used for each rune verse in this book unless otherwise stated.

How to use this book

This book is designed to be both an interesting read and a personal journey for those who wish to learn about runes, primarily the English runes. It is about runic magic and magical experience containing practical exercises to deepen your connection. Wyrd, an early English word for the concept of connection with all of life, is especially important in this journey. There are many suggestions on experiential ways you can use to connect to the people who first used the English runes.

My hope is that through the thoughts and explorations you find in this book you will gain your own personal connection to these runes. Every so often I will be asking you to make notes so I suggest you find a note book or journal to record your thoughts and experiences; however disconnected they may seem at the time. This journal will become an invaluable resource on your journey to find your own personal connection with each individual rune and the magic that surrounds them. There is a companion journal 'The English Runes: *Study Journal'* available for this purpose as well as a personal divination journal 'The English Runes: *Rune of the Day Journal'*.

Suzanne Rance
Sussex, England
Spring 2017

Part 1

Runes and

The English Runes

Runes and their history

The runes are a form of alphabet: each rune has both an individual sound and a specific name. It is said that knowing the name of something/someone gives you power over it/them; a concept that occurs in historical cultures from ancient Egypt and the Americas, and can be found in the Bible and the folklore of many lands. No one is certain why each rune has an independent name and meaning, so, although all writing in the ancient world held power, the naming of runes seems to enhance their power above all other alphabets used in European society.

Runes as we understand them today are believed to have been formed during the period c.250 BCE to 150 CE; however, potential earlier instances can be dated back as far as 1300 BCE. Ancient rock markings with visible similarities to runes can be found across the Eurasian continent and were carved using straight lines, but archaeologists are yet to find conclusive proof that these are early runes.

Today people use the runes for divination and spell casting, and this is not new. It is believed their original use was for casting lots and for divination. Cornelius Tacitus (58-120 CE), Consul to the region of Germania in about 97 CE, recorded a Germanic tribal 'Runemal' in Chapter 10 of his ethnographical work *Germania*.

> *To divination they pay much attention. Their method is a simple one: they cut a branch from a fruit-bearing tree and divide it into small pieces which they mark with certain distinctive signs and scatter at random onto a white cloth. Then the priest of the community (if it is done publicly) or the father of the family (if it is done privately) after invoking the gods and with eyes raised to heavens, picks up three pieces one at a time and interprets them in accordance with the signs previously marked on them.*
> Cornelius Tacitus

Runes were used for inscriptional purposes. Early forms, scratched on various bits of wood, metal, stone and bone, have been found preserved from Greece to Greenland. There are also runic graffiti: runes were carved on the inside walls of Maeshowe, Orkney, when it was used for shelter by the Vikings in the 12th century; they left graffiti such as 'Ofram the son of Sigurd carved these runes', 'Tholfir Kolbeinsson carved these runes high up' and, carved beside a drawing of a dog, 'Ingigerth is the most beautiful of all women'.

The runes rarely occur in manuscripts and most inscriptions are brief, consisting only of a few words or sentences at most, usually in poems and riddles. Runes and Latin letters were both considered capable of multiple functions: for example, as a means of communication and of holding magical power; the 10th-century poem 'Solomon and Saturn' is an example of this, with the Latin letters being accompanied by runes to spell out the opening words of the Lord's Prayer in Latin: *Pater Noster*.

Where does the name 'rune' come from?

The word itself has ancient roots that may be traced back to the Proto-Indo-European word *rew*, which means to roar, murmur, mumble or whisper; it may be the root of the following:

Old English

Rún - a whisper, a confidence, council, consultation
Rún - *stæf* - runic letter
Rún - *cræftig* - skilled in explaining mysteries

Old Norse

Rún - mystery, secret knowledge, magical sign, runic character

Old Irish

Rún - secret, mystery

Middle Welsh

Rhin - magic charm

Old English runes and their relationship to the Elder Futhark

Old English runes are just that: English! Also known as the Anglo Saxon Futhorc or Anglo-Frisian Rune Row these runes were all used in England but not all used in Frisia (an ancient region of north-west Europe that corresponds roughly to modern provinces in the Netherlands and north-west Germany). This indicates that English changes are already present in this rune row and that there is also the possibility that our Futhorc was passed to Frisia.

The Old English runes are the sound of the Old English language and as such the sound of the birth of modern English. The English language developed out of a Proto-Germanic or Common Germanic language, which in turn developed from a Proto-Indo-European one. The sound of English has changed so much it is hardly recognisable and it continues to develop even now.

Changes from the earlier Common Germanic language can be found in the name 'Futhorc': the first letters of the rune row, just like 'A', 'B' and 'C', are the first letters of the alphabet. The reason the Old English runes are called 'Futhorc' and not 'Futhark' like the Elder Runes is due to vowel and consonantal sound changes as the language developed. This, coupled with other pronunciation changes, explains why there are 29 runes in *The Old English Rune Poem*, or *OERP*, as opposed to 24 in the Elder Futhark. There are a few additional runes that you may be familiar with written at the bottom of the oldest remaining manuscript for the *OERP* below. Runes such as Stan and Gar are known as the Northumbrian Runes but, as they do not have verses in the *OERP*, they will not be included in this book.

The *OERP* gives a positive historical framework and meaning to these runes that goes right back into the Early Middle Ages, and probably earlier than that. It is thought to be an abecedarium, or medieval teaching aid. Each letter would have had a symbolic meaning and all letters possessed supernatural power. The original dialect is not known for certain but it is likely that it had some southern English, possibly Kentish, origin, although the majority of it is more likely West Saxon.

The Elder Futhark is the oldest known rune row and there is a database, created by Kiel University for their Rune Project that lists all the Elder Futhark finds up to 2012. It notes all of the places where the runes were found and shows that the modern countries these texts have been recovered from are: Austria, Belgium, Bosnia-Herzegovina, Czech Republic, Denmark, France, Germany, Hungary, Norway, Netherlands, Poland, Romania, Russia, Sweden, Switzerland and Ukraine (none in the UK).

The Elder Futhark is often chosen by pagans and heathens because it is the oldest and therefore seems to be the obvious choice. Consider this though: yes, there is an Elder Futhark script and, yes, this was the script first used, but we would not have a clue about its meaning without the written evidence of Old English, Norwegian and Icelandic rune poems. There is no evidence of an original Germanic rune poem and of the three surviving poems the oldest and richest source is the *OERP*.

The Old English runes carry within them the meanings of the Elder Futhark but there are subtle differences and some new runic characters. The *OERP* is seen by academics to be the oldest of the surviving rune poems, c.10th or 11th century, with language suggesting it may predate that; it is older than *The Norwegian Rune Poem* (13th century) and *The Icelandic Rune Poem* (15th century), but linguists have used all three to decipher the characters of the Elder Futhark.

Academics have studied the *OERP* for years so that Old English can be understood. Tolkien studied the language and these runes; he called them the 'English runes' and used them as the basis for the runes in *The Hobbit* and the inspiration for his other rune rows. With all this history and knowledge at our fingertips it is time to step up and be proud of the 'English runes' and ensure they take their place in magical practice.

The Old English Rune Poem manuscript

The Old English Rune Poem (*OERP*) manuscript (MS Cotton Ortho B. x. fol. 165), was destroyed in the Cottonian Library fire of 1731, but fortunately a scholar named George Hickes had printed the poem in the 'Grammatica Anglo-Saxonica' of his thesaurus.

There have been arguments about who owned the manuscript, who added the rune names and even if the rune staves were on the original. Perhaps the original medieval scribe transcribed the poem including only the rune staves with the verses and later an Old English scribe added the names of the runes as a gloss.

The manuscript has been traced back to Tudor times when it is believed to have belonged to John Joscelyn (1529-1603), a keen collector of old manuscripts. It definitely became part of the Cottonian Library, a private collection belonging to Sir Robert Bruce Cotton MP (1571-1631), an antiquarian and bibliophile whose library became the basis of the British Library.

The manuscript was subsequently studied by George Hickes (1642-1715), a bishop and antiquarian. Hickes entered Oxford in 1659, studying at St John's College and Magdalen College. In 1673 he graduated in Divinity, and in 1675 he was appointed rector of St Ebbe's, Oxford. He is known today for his work on *Institutiones Grammaticae Anglo-Saxonicae et Moeso-Gothicae* (1689) and later *Linguarum Veterum Septentrionalium*

Runes and the English Runes

Thesaurus (1703-05), a comparative grammar of Old English and the related Germanic tongues.

The Old English Rune Poem; a facsimile of the oldest surviving copy

In 'Hickes's Additions to the Runic Poem', *Modern Philology* 1, by Hempl, G. (1903/4), Hempl goes a long way towards proving that the rune values and several variant names found in Hickes' poem are borrowed from MS Cotton Domitian A. ix. F. 11 which Hickes reproduced on the page after the *OERP*. He gives further evidence that this was when the rune names were added to the facsimile and that the copy was actually made by Humphrey Wanley (Oxford, 1705), although no one knows which manuscript he obtained the names from.

MS Cotton Domitian A. ix. F. 11 (facsimile)

The Elder Futhark or the Old English Futhorc

Here are some points in favour of considering English runes from *The Old English Rune Poem* instead of the Common Germanic Elder Futhark:

- From an academic view we know so much more about the Old English language than we do about the Common Germanic language.

- Common Germanic, also known as Proto-Germanic, is a language that has been reconstructed using Old English and other descendent languages.

- England has many Old English manuscripts by famous and prolific writers such as King Alfred and the Venerable Bede:

people straight out of our history books whose writing helps to inform us about how life really was.

- The Old English language has *Beowulf*, which is full of amazing descriptions of early English life and beliefs that enrich our knowledge of pre-Christian times.

- *The Old English Rune Poem* with its illumination of the meanings of the English runes is the oldest of the surviving rune poems; there is no evidence for an earlier Elder Futhark poem.

- In recent years more evidence about the early English has been uncovered.

- Today we have increasingly well-researched books about the early English peoples and the society they lived in.

The Old English Rune Poem and the life of the early English

The Old English Rune Poem (OERP) is a window into early English life: a life that was less mechanised than ours today and where everything including the unseen was palpable. The early English lived in smaller groups around a central social building known now as the feast hall and known then as, among other names, the *beorsele* ('beer cellar' in modern English). Imagine yourself in a place with no street lights, no cars and no supermarkets, where you have to grow your own food, make your own clothes and even make the cloth before you can make those clothes. The dark is dark and the marshes can swallow you whole; people can disappear and this is often due to the known and unknown creatures and monsters beyond the boundaries of your homestead.

I am using two translations of the *OERP*; the first translation is from Stephen Pollington's *Rudiments of Rune Lore (1995)* and the second is from John M. Kemble's essay on Anglo-Saxon Runes published in the journal *Archaeologia (1840)*. Both translations are correct but they are separated in time by 150 years. In his essay Kemble wrote that he was unaware of any English translation of the OERP and that Wilhelm Grimm's German translation was inaccurate, so Kemble's English translation is likely the oldest that we have. With new technologies our understanding of the early English culture has developed considerably during these 150 years and can be seen in how differently the language is used and how the verses are viewed by these two scholars of the Old English language. As you become more familiar with the poem you will be able to add your own understanding.

There are many ways to learn about the English Runes and what they mean to you; part two is designed to help you to discover and build your own relationship with each rune: to find out how the runes speak to you. To help you with your discovery I have included the poem one verse at a time, first in Old English and then in modern English. Each rune will be accompanied by some facts, musings and deductions about its meaning. These are to help you come to your own conclusions and are my own interpretations based on how the poem speaks to me. Some of the verses will seem easy while others will appear more like riddles. There is a distinct possibility that each verse was once a riddle and was sung in the feast hall, with the audience joining in to find the answers. Maybe it was sung one verse at a time, without the rune name, followed by different people in the audience being put on the spot as they tried to work out its name and meaning.

Learning the Old English runes

Learning the Old English runes should not be a race and it should be more than a book exercise; if you make the effort to gradually absorb them you will find it worthwhile. I recommend you study the poem by making an effort to mentally walk in the footsteps of the early English, accessing information about their society in the way that suits you best. You may choose to look at research on archaeological finds, or visit Anglo-Saxon sites such as Sutton Hoo, and reconstructed villages such as West Stow in the UK. If you are unable to visit, you may find that meeting re-enactment groups at shows and fairs will help. There are videos on the internet and some very well-researched fiction on the lives of people such as King Alfred. If you love non-fiction as much as I do, there are increasing numbers of books with the latest views on early English life: the publisher Anglo-Saxon Books offers very good resources. Also, don't forget documentaries; there are lots available on TV, and channels such as the History Channel are a rich resource. Look for the latest theories and see what wonderful insights they may contain.

Keep a journal; this is a must and will become an invaluable personal reference, there is a companion Study Journal available for this book. Try

Runes and the English Runes

to study one rune at a time, maybe one a week. Draw it, read its verse, keep a picture of the rune under your pillow or paint it on your body. Try singing the rune - tips for which can be found this later in this book - and make sure you keep your journal updated with all of your feelings and thoughts about the individual runes. The companion Study Journal is sectioned providing several pages for each rune so that you can add new thoughts and ideas as you develop your understanding of and relationship with each rune. Alternatively you could also use an exercise book or a loose leaf folder. Listen to the sound of Old English and learn how the runes are pronounced. There is a great website that features spoken recordings of everything that has been written in Old English. It is called Anglo-Saxon Aloud and has been produced by Michael D. C. Drout, Prentice Professor of English at Wheaton College, Norton, MA. The website includes a recording called 'Rune Poem', and can be found here: http://acadblogs.wheatoncollege.edu/mdrout

This way of learning the English runes will be quite a long journey, as there are 29 of them, but to accompany the longer, in-depth learning I suggest you should also have some fun. For this you will need runes so if you haven't any yet you can draw them on separate pieces of paper and fold them like raffle tickets or find some small stones and a permanent marker. First thing in the morning you can pull a 'rune of the day' out of your bag; there is a companion Rune of the Day Journal available for this exercise or, as with the Study Journal, you can use any writing book. First look at the poem and musings in this book and note them down then, at the end of the day see how the rune you have picked enlightens and enlivens your experience of the day. Did anything happen today that you can associate with the rune? Perhaps an opportunity arrived and the rune alluded to it. Another way is to ask the runes a question for guidance and see how the rune you choose relates to this question; you may not think it has a connection to start with, but, gradually, as your knowledge deepens, you will become aware of it. Beware though, runes are not as complex as tarot cards and sometimes they can be very blunt in their responses; however, later in this book you will find out how to expand your readings.

So it is time to move onto the individual runes. The order of the *OERP* is thought to be the original order and, although there has been plenty of discussion about this, there is a very good argument for the fact that the *OERP* was copied unaltered from the original document. The order also falls in line with the Elder Futhark, which was set in stone: the Kylver Stone in Gotland, in 400 CE, to be precise.

Part 2

The Futhorc

Feoh - Wealth

*Feoh byþ frofur fira gehwylcum;
sceal ðeah manna gehwylc miclun hyt dælan
gif he wile for drihtne domes hleotan.*

Wealth is a comfort to any man
yet each person must share it out well
if he wants to win a good name before his lord.

This rune has the phonemic value /f/, as in friend, but when used in the middle of the word becomes a /v/, as in seven. As Old English is a phonetic language you always pronounce an 'H' at the end of a word. 'H' can be pronounced like the 'H' in house or as a very soft-throated 'ch', like the Scottish word 'loch' but softer. This rune is pronounced 'fay-och'.

Feoh is translated as 'cattle'. They were seen as movable wealth and this is the interpretation given to Fehu in the Elder Futhark. In fact, cattle were the world's first and oldest form of money; they included cows, camels, goats and other animals. Cattle enabled the seller to set their price, which is thought to have created an early form of standard pricing: two goats had the price of one cow; therefore cows were twice as valuable as goats. To the early English, Feoh represented money, wealth, or even treasure. Early coins have been found in parts of southern England and the first coins used in Britain were imported from the Belgi[c]a. The Belgae were a Celtic tribe from northern France who settled in what is now the south-east of England and the first coins were minted in Britain around 80 BCE. So Feoh could have been gold, silver, ships, food, lodging or anything that a person could barter with. Interestingly, trading in cattle and the need for account-keeping is believed to have been responsible for the development of writing. This helps makes sense of the use of Feoh as the first letter in the runic alphabet and, although no one really knows for certain, it could be more than just a coincidence.

This verse advises that wealth is a comfort but should be shared, especially if you want a good name. Anyone keeping their wealth to themselves will become distanced from society and be deemed the poorer in spirit for it. The Old English culture prized sharing very highly and hospitality was offered to anyone who came by. Consequently, if you wanted those you held in high regard to think well of you, sharing out your wealth was the appropriate thing to do, even if you could not afford to do so.

> *Money is a consolation to every man;*
> *yet shall every man liberally distribute it,*
> *if he will that, before God, honour shall fall to his lot.*
> Kemble

Kemble's translation uses 'shall fall to his lot' for *hleotan*, which means both 'the casting of lots' and 'to receive by appointment/be appointed to', the latter being a recognition from an authority. The Old English were keen to influence their 'lot in life': their standing in society and recognition by others. It was very important to be remembered for your deeds after death and the wandering bard or *scop* would sing tales of famous ancestors. Being open-handed and generous to strangers and friends alike was a way to influence your lot, and it was soon noticed if you did not behave in this way.

Kemble sees the word *drihtne* as 'God'; however, a more direct translation would be 'lord', who for the early English would have been the leader of their tribal group. The rune poem was first written down by monks and took place in a church scriptorium where the Christian God would have been their lord of choice. The importance of the Christian God became paramount in a land that was changing from small communities with a local king into a land where a sole king ruled over the country as God's representative, a land where everyone was required to value one God and one king. Both the king and the Church were becoming stronger and they required funds from the people by way of taxes in order to hold that strength. These taxes could be taken in coin, treasure or food from the harvest: any movable wealth or Feoh.

So what does Feoh mean to you?

Consider what wealth means. Have a good think about it, meditate, or go for a walk. The poem says wealth creates comfort for men and women, but to be well thought of by your peers you must share what you have. Wealth comes in many forms; it can be anything you can barter or swap. Could you extend it to encompass your creative ability, your ability to heal others, or the fact that you are a good listener? This rune can signify material wealth – lack of it, or glut – and it can point out responsibilities that come with wealth of any kind. In your journal create a list of all of the things that you consider to be wealth and the possible feelings that accompany these. If you are short of money consider how you would feel if you were wealthy; would it really solve your problems or would it distance you from others? How do people cope if they have no monetary wealth? It may be that they have a number of other skills that can help them out, such as the musical ability needed for busking.

Ūr - Aurochs

Ūr byþ anmod ond oferhyrned,
felafrecne deor, feohteþ mid hornum
mǣre morstapa; þæt is modig wuht.

Aurochs is fierce and high-horned
the courageous beast fights with its horns
a well-known moor-treader, it is a brave creature.

This rune has the phonemic value /u/, as in boo, and the beginning vowel in this word is long. To pronounce long vowels in Old English you make the same sound but hold it for longer: that is, the sound itself doesn't change. The 'R' is thought to have been trilled or rolled; if you can't roll your 'R's, try pronouncing them without your teeth closed instead.

The aurochs ranged the moors and fens alone and the verse highlights this aspect of the animal as well the fact that it was a fearless fighter: both male and female aurochs were known for their fighting habits. For these reasons the aurochs were held in high regard by the early societies whose paths they crossed. Caesar wrote about the use of the aurochs in the territories of Germania:

> ... those animals which are called uri. These are a little below the elephant in size, and of the appearance, colour, and shape of a bull. Their strength and speed are extraordinary; they spare neither man nor wild beast which they have espied. These the Germans take with much pains in pits and kill them. The young men harden themselves with this exercise, and practice themselves in this sort of hunting, and those who have slain the greatest number of them, having produced the horns in public, to serve as evidence, receive great praise. But not even when taken very young can they be rendered familiar to men and tamed. The size, shape, and appearance of their horns differ much from the horns of our oxen. These they anxiously seek after, and bind at

The Futhorc

the tips with silver, and use as cups at their most sumptuous entertainments.
Julius Caesar's 'The Gallic War' Book 6, Chapter. 28.

We can see from Caesar's description above that there was a great admiration for the aurochs among our Germanic ancestors. Although aurochs were no longer found in Britain, having died out during the early Bronze Age, they were still widespread in mainland Europe during the time of the Roman Empire. It is clear the Romans admired their size, strength and ferocity, and they were widely popular as a battle beast in their great amphitheatres. Reports say aurochs were not scared of humans and tended to ignore them with a disdainful demeanour, but if they were teased or hunted they became very aggressive and dangerous and could throw the perpetrators high into the air.

Kemble uses the word 'bull' instead of 'aurochs', but it is believed he meant an aurochs bull. There is no meaningful difference between these two translations.

Bull is fierce and horned above,
the very bold beast fighteth with horns,
a mighty stepper over the moors: that is a courageous creature.
Kemble

Aurochs weren't just important to the Germanic peoples: they were worshipped as sacred animals in Anatolia (modern Turkey) and the Near East during the Iron Age. They were shown as the lunar bull, associated with the great goddess Cybele and later the bull in the Mithras cult. It is likely that excessive hunting was the cause of their extinction and by the 13th century they existed only in small numbers in Eastern Europe, where hunting of aurochs became a privilege of nobles and, later, royal households.

The aurochs was kept in the Futhorc and *The Old English Rune Poem* as part of early English traditional lore. Fighting the aurochs was seen as an ancient rite of passage into manhood and to drink from an aurochs horn may have been seen as a way of passing on the vigour both of the animal and the young man who won the prize. Bull-leaping was an ancient rite across Europe – especially in Anatolia and Minoan Crete – and the remains of large aurochs drinking horns were found at the Sutton Hoo ship burial in Suffolk, England.

Anton Schneeberger, a 16th-century Swiss botanist and naturalist, studied the aurochs in Poland and reported that although they roamed alone, during the winter they formed single-sex herds of no more than 30 animals. Schneeberger was one of the last naturalists to be able to observe the aurochs in life and most of our knowledge is gained from him.

So what does Ur mean to you?

The verse quite clearly speaks of bravery and the high horns seem to express a feeling of pride and confidence. It is always a good thing to read these verses singly when you are relaxed, and to meditate on them and try to visualise the scene. On the internet you can find information about the aurochs, which was still seen, although rarely, during Anton Schneeberger's time. What about the aurochs as a sign of adulthood, a rite of passage? The extract from Caesar's writings above tells us that the young men hunted and fought with the aurochs to harden themselves. When applying this to the rune it can signify a teenager, not necessarily male, a rite of passage and/or bravery.

In his book, *The Old Ways*, Robert MacFarlane highlights indigenous societies where wisdom is laid down by creating paths and you can find various instances where humans follow animals - not for hunting, but to learn the secrets of their survival and how these may help their own tribes. In the north, where the winter is long, people would study the local bears to enable them to find food: as they could eat the same things as bears, people could emulate them in what they ate to build fat stores and by storing what they could. Could the aurochs have been such an animal? It could be associated with a time away from others, your friends or family, where you need to tread a lonely path and fend for yourself, where you gain wisdom laid down by those gone before. Note everything in your journal; look back on your own life and see what you may have learned under similar circumstances.

The Futhorc

Þorn - Thorn

Þorn byþ ðearle scearp; ðegna gehwylcum
anfeng ys yfyl, ungemetum reþe
manna gehwelcum, ðe him mid resteð

Thorn is painfully sharp to any warrior
seizing it is bad, excessively severe
for any person who lays among them.

This rune has the phonemic value /θ/, which is pronounced 'th', as in thorn, not forgetting to roll the 'R' of course. When used in the middle of the word it becomes a /ð/, which is 'th', as in that.

I have to admit that every time I read this stanza I think of Sleeping Beauty and the following description, which is from one of the earliest translations into English of the story collected by M. M. Grimm.

> A large hedge of thorns soon grew round the palace, and every year it became higher and thicker, till at last the whole palace was surrounded and hid, so that not even the roof or the chimneys could be seen. But there went a report through all the land of the beautiful sleeping Rose-Bud (for so was the king's daughter called): so that from time to time several kings' sons came, and tried to break through the thicket into the palace. This they could never do; for the thorns and bushes laid hold of them as it were with hands, and there they stuck fast and died miserably.
> 'Rose-Bud' from Kinder- und Haus-Märchen

A young prince heard the story from an old man and despite the old man's warnings decided he would go and find Rose-Bud.

> Now that very day were the hundred years completed; and as the prince came to the thicket, he saw nothing but beautiful flowing

shrubs, through which he passed with ease, and they closed after him as firm as ever.
'Rose-Bud' from Kinder- und Haus-Märchen, first published in 1812 and translated by Edgar Taylor (1793-1839), also called Grimm's Fairy Tales, Collected by M. M. Grimm from Oral Tradition

Thorn is very sharp to every man,
bad to take hold of, immeasurably severe
to every man that resteth with him.
Kemble

Both translations say much the same thing but it has been argued that, of all the runes, this is the one most likely to have been changed by the development of Christianity. Þurs (Thurs) is believed to have been its original name; this name is included in *The Norwegian Rune Poem*, in which the Old Norse rune Þurs is a demon/giant. Although the evidence for this is younger than *The Old English Rune Poem*, it can be argued that *The Norwegian Rune Poem* is pre-Christian and that the verse makes sense if you use demon or giant instead of thorn. If we look at Grendel in *Beowulf*, we find a demon who wounds or kills everyone who tries to seize him and several times he kills those who are sleeping in Heorot (the name of the king's mead-hall), which is near to where he lives.

In the Rose-Bud story you can see the thorn hedge has correlations with the giants: something in nature that is very large and has been placed to stand guard around the sleeping princess and her entourage. This giant kills, in a miserable way, anyone who tries to get past it. It has been set there by magic and only at the allotted time will it allow the chosen prince to pass. There were many beings lurking in nature and they were known to grab unsuspecting people and take them to their death; they could be water spirits who would drown you or giants who would batter you, pull you apart and perhaps throw you from cliffs. To the early English the world was full of these beings; they lived at a time when all life had a spirit and soul, including plants, bodies of water, rocks and caves. These were known as wights or *wiht* in Old English.

This verse clearly tells us that thorn is very unpleasant, conjuring feelings that can be understood by anyone who has tried to pick fruit or a rose from a thorny bush. I don't think any of us would willingly grab hold of or sit among thorns: the wounds are surprisingly painful for their size. Gardeners are warned about roses and their link with tetanus. In fact, any minor damage, such as a scratch from a thorn, can cause us severe harm if the tetanus bacterium enters it, given that tetanus is 50 times as poisonous as cobra venom.

So what does Þorn mean to you?

Today we are advised to get to the doctors for an infected thorn wound but what about the effect of the thorn on the early societies? Seeing the hidden strength of thorns can open our eyes to their effects and, bearing this in mind, do you think that the name of this rune has been changed? Do you think there is a chance that thorns and dangerous beings could in fact be the same thing? Meditate on and perhaps research the animistic nature attributed to plants in different cultures: perhaps this could also be applied to the beliefs of the early English. Perhaps the rune has a meaning that is hidden from us by time? As you learn about what this rune means to you, think about how this meaning could be applied both as a protection, as in the story of Rose-Bud, or as a threat and a warning against unseen harm.

Ōs - God

Ōs byþ ordfruma ælcre spræce,
wisdomes wraþu ond witena frofur
and eorla gehwam eadnys ond tohiht.

God is the origin of all language
wisdom's foundation and wise man's comfort
and to every hero blessing and hope.

This rune has the phonemic value of /o/, pronounced as the 'O' in orange, and you can see from the bar across the 'Ō' that it is a long vowel.

Ōs translates as 'god', not the Christian God but one of the *Ese* (Old English for Aesir, Norse ruling gods) and the rune itself differs in shape from the one in the same place within the Elder Futhark. This is due to a sound change but this rune still holds the same meaning as the original rune, whose shape still exists in the Anglo-Frisian Futhorc as Æsc with the phonemic value of /æ/: 'A' as in apple.

The god this rune represents is thought to be Woden who brought the runes to the world. The Woden of the English shares a lot with, but does not appear to be the same as, Odin the 'All-Father' of the Norse gods. He is primarily a god of frenzy and his name has its roots in the Proto-Germanic word *wodaz*, which is related to Latin *vātēs* and Old Irish *fáith*, both meaning 'seer'; other words that stem from *wodaz* include Old English *wōd* (mad), Gothic *woþs* (possessed) and Old Norse *óðr* (mad, frantic, furious). To the early English, Woden held a particular place as an ancestral figure in royal genealogies. This association with the genealogies certainly gives rise to Woden being a father figure but he seems to be more ancient than Odin. There are several hundred years between Odin, the All-Father, and Woden, who existed before the idea of the one god took hold in the northern realms. Odin needed to stand up to the God of Christianity by being bigger, better and, to be honest, a bit more sophisticated. Out of frenzy comes inspiration and the fact that the Romans equated Woden with Mercury suggests that he was indeed a god of eloquence. In addition, there is of course battle frenzy, which gives advantage to the winning side and so associates him as a god of victory in battle.

Woden was especially known to the early English as the leader of the Wild Hunt, a group of supernatural huntsmen who collected souls. This gives him the role of a psychopomp and often he was seen as a one-eyed wanderer with a long grey beard, a long coat and a staff, who stopped at crossroads to collect the souls of the dead. The early English often buried their babies at crossroads, knowing that Woden would pass by and that he would care for them and take their souls to another life.

I mentioned that Woden also brought the runes to the world, and, although there are no early English stories to corroborate this, he certainly held an important association with them. In the 8th century CE the Venerable Bede records the use of runes to loosen the shackles on Imma after the Battle of Trent in 679. The story tells that every time they tried to put on restraints they fell off. Imma was asked if he knew loosening runes and if he was keeping the staves hidden on him; it is very likely that this relates to the charm mentioned by Odin in the later Icelandic book the *Hávamál*. The Venerable Bede recognises the miracle of this but he obviously gives the credit to God. Runes also feature in the 'Nine Herbs Charm'; this is found in the Old English collection of herbal remedies, charms and prayers known as *The Lacnunga*, which dates from the 10th century CE, possibly earlier. It says:

Wyrm com snican, toslat he man.
Þa genam Woden VIIII wuldortanas,
Sloh ða þa naeddran þat heo on VIIII tofleah.'

A worm came crawling, he tore a man apart,
then Woden took up nine glory-rods,
struck the adder then so it flew apart into nine.
Pollington, Stephen
Leechcraft *Early English Charms Plantlore and Healing* (2000)

The *wuldortanas* or glory-rods are believed by the academics to be rune sticks and here Woden clearly has full magical knowledge of their powers.

Kemble uses the word 'mouth' as his translation of Ōs, and this is the Latin meaning of the word. Mouth is possibly chosen because Ōs is not used in the Old English Bible to mean God and it fits in well with the verse.

> *Mouth is the origin of every speech,*
> *The support of wisdom, and comfort of councillors,*
> *And to every man blessing and confidence*
> Kemble

The Latin meaning of Ōs may have helped in concealing the presence of the god Woden from the monks, or at least in allowing its use in *The Old English Rune Poem*. Perhaps Woden was not the All-Father Odin, but he was still an important God to the early English, as attested by the number of place names related to his name. For this reason the Church is likely to have forbidden the use of his name in order to reduce his importance to the people. The word Ōs only appears in the *Bosworth-Toller Anglo-Saxon Dictionary* as the rune name Ōs, but the fact that it forms part of many Old English names suggests that it was well known. A name such as Osgar (Oscar) literally means 'god spear' (the spear of god) or 'divine spear'; Osric is 'god ruler' (the ruler chosen by god) or 'divine ruler'; and there are also the names Oswald, Oswine, and Oswiu. Such names show there was a lasting tradition for the meaning and use of Ōs which very likely pre-dates the Christian era.

So what does Ōs mean to you?

We can see from the verses that the interpretations 'god' and 'mouth' hold true. Which meaning do you prefer? If Ōs is Woden, the god of victory and frenzy, the wise one who can be consulted by those who are able, he would have been seen as a blessing and a joy to all believers, and for those who defended their family or tribe he would have been the source of strength to do that.

Perhaps this rune says both to you; this can sometimes offer a wider meaning, depending on how you wish to employ Ōs. For further inspiration you could perhaps visit a crossroads – not a busy one on a suburban street, but one on an old trackway. Here you can quietly talk to the god Woden and ask for inspiration about this rune: what it means and how it relates to the other runes. For a great modern view of Woden, you could read *American Gods* by Neil Gaiman, who shows how the gods travel with the people who believe in them and even includes a main character called Mr Wednesday (Wodensday).

Rād – Riding

ᚱ

*Rād byþ on recyde rinca gehwylcum
sefte ond swiþhwæt, ðamðe sitteþ on ufan
meare mægenheardum ofer milpaþas.*

Riding is for every man in the hall
easy, and strenuous for him who sits upon
a powerful horse along the long paths.

This rune has the phonemic value /r/, as in ride and, as mentioned in Ūr, it was trilled or rolled in Old English. The rune is pronounced 'rād', with a long vowel sounding somewhere between 'ah' and 'oar'; its phonemic value is /ɔː/, as you will see in the rune Ac.

Rād means riding: that is, riding on a horse or in a cart; it is also the name of the paths where the riding takes place, for example *þunor-rád* (in modern English, 'Thor's Road'). At first this verse seems a little confusing – I mean, who goes riding in a hall? Are they just boasting about how effortless it is to journey from place to place on their horses? Perhaps the verse is telling us that however much everyone boasts about how easy it is, reality bites and it is always more strenuous than you remember. On the other hand, when we look at Kemble's translation he names Rād as 'saddle', which seems very different but just as confusing.

> Saddle is in the house to every man
> soft and very bold, for him that sitteth upon
> the very strong horse, over the mile paths.
> **Kemble**

This verse can be seen as a riddle – the early English loved them – and although confusing to us, it is not so difficult when you understand that the word *rād* had several meanings. Riding and road have been mentioned but it also has the further meaning of furniture in a building and furniture on a horse, namely the harness and saddle. When this verse was originally heard the name of the rune was not vocalised or seen, the only clue would be 'in the hall furniture is comfortable, soft and easy to sit upon, but you have to be braver to sit on a horse for miles'; this leads to the word *rād*, which had the primary meaning of 'riding' to the early English.

Riding and travel go hand in hand; with a horse you can travel further and faster than with a cart you can carry heavier loads. Humans have been travelling since the beginning of our time: moving to new hunting areas, following animals, finding new territories and also travelling to meet up with other tribal groups in the same wider family. School gave me the impression that historical peoples stayed in one place and certainly didn't travel over long distances, then in 2002 archaeologists discovered the Amesbury Archer not far from Stonehenge. Isotope tests were carried out on his teeth and they discovered it was likely he originally came from the Alps in Central Europe.

It appears humans have always felt the need to travel and the early English were no different. English warriors travelled as far as Byzantium, now Istanbul, and were found among the Varangian Guard, bodyguards to the Byzantine emperor. Those who travelled within England included the *scops*, musicians and storytellers, who would travel from hall to hall, not only providing entertainment but also picking up and passing on news. Not everyone could travel as far as the warriors or *scops*, as there were farms that needed to be tended and homes that needed protection, but travel was still important. At certain times of the year farmers would take their wagons with any surplus crops and drive their animals to market; these were either bartered for things that they could not make or grow themselves or exchanged for coin and other precious metals.

So what does Rād mean to you?

This rune offers a few meanings, mostly around the road, riding or travel and – oddly – furnishings. How do you feel about the latter? It does seem very strange but maybe less so when associated with travel. Have you ever travelled a long way in something that is not too comfortable? I think we can all see that travelling in a brand new top-of-the-range car over a long distance is likely to be a lot more comfortable than in an older cheaper car – after all, first-class seating has far better upholstery than economy class.

The Futhorc

One secret to finding the meaning or meanings of this rune is to think about your own travels. Perhaps you have travelled a long way from home. When you look back at it now, have you forgotten the discomforts? Have you ever experienced a journey where you said 'never again', but after a few weeks or months found yourself tempted to do something similar? There is also the phrase 'to travel hopefully is a better thing than to arrive'. Do you think this rune could carry this message within it? What about travelling along life's path? Do you know someone who has set out to follow one career and then come to a crossroads and chosen another path? There are some people who like to take opportunities that are offered to them even when this takes them from a seemingly rewarding path. Don't forget to add your thoughts to your journal.

Cēn - Torch

ᚳ

*Cēn byþ cwicera gehwam, cuþ on fyre
blac ond beorhtlic, byrneþ oftust
ðær hi æþelingas inne restaþ.*

*Torch is known to each living being by fire
radiant and bright, it usually burns
where nobles rest indoors.*

This rune has the phonemic value /k/, or a 'C' as in cake. The rune is pronounced 'kane' with an extended 'A', which is like the 'E' in 'eh', but a longer sound. This rune also has a different shape to Kenaz, the rune that is in this place in the Elder Futhark.

The verse that accompanies Torch seems pretty straightforward. Most have been lucky enough to sit by a roaring fire and seen how it lights the area, radiant and bright. If we were to take ourselves back 1500 years or more we would see torches in the halls where the nobles rest. Torches tended to be used for lighting large spaces and corridors during the early English period; in smaller spaces people were more likely to have used candles made of tallow. A torch was made out of a pine or fir stick that was saturated with turpentine, a distillation of resin from live pine trees. These torches would have burned well and turpentine is pretty combustible, so it would have made quite a bright light that didn't go out easily.

> *Torch is to all living, well known on fire,
> pale and bright it oftenest burneth,
> where the nobles rest them within.*
> Kemble

Kemble's translation differs slightly: he describes the light as pale while Pollington translates it as radiant. It appears to be a small difference but once again we are confronted with a word meaning different things. The word here is *blac*; in the *Bosworth-Toller Anglo-Saxon Dictionary* it has two meanings:

1. bright, shining;
2. bleak, pale, pallid, livid, as in death.

Old English has many words that mean different things but for this verse it is more likely to be 'bright, shining or radiant' because if you investigate you will find that turpentine burns too fiercely for use in an enclosed vessel such as a lamp. Of course as with other runes there is sometimes an element of riddling and the use of one meaning while highlighting the other.

Blæc is another spelling of *blac*, and is slightly different in its pronunciation, but if you look at this spelling it broadens the interpretation to include black and bleach, once again expanding the meaning of the rune to include both dark and light, perhaps even from dark to light.

This rune is usually popularised as signifying 'to know' or 'knowing', as is the case in the Elder Futhark, but this meaning is difficult to find in earlier Old English prior to the Viking invasion. Kenna, 'to know or perceive', can be found in Old Norse and it has survived into Scottish and northern English dialects as ken, 'to know, understand'. It can be found in West Frisian *kenne*, 'to know, recognise'; in Dutch *kennen*, 'to know'; and in German *kennen*, 'to know or be acquainted with'. Cēn is not found as a word in its own right in the Old English texts we have remaining but if we expand our search there are a couple of slightly different words starting with Cen/Cēn, both with and without the long ē sound. The *Bosworth-Toller Anglo-Saxon Dictionary* offers:

- Cennan: *to beget, conceive, create, bring forth*, which can be said of knowledge;
- Cēne: *keen, fierce, bold, brave, warlike*; here the spelling is the same as Cēn but with an added syllable at the end, like kane-uh.

These extra words make a translation of 'knowledge and bravery' feasible, with ideas and knowledge being conceived in the hall and fierce, bold, brave or warlike deeds being boasted about by nobles and warriors in the hall.

So what does Cēn mean to you?

Cēn as a torch is fairly easy to interpret: it is an instrument of light and illumination, of being able to see in dark places; this light can be pale or bright and, as the poem says, everyone knows this. Do you think this can be extended into knowledge? Is this another riddle verse? After all, to become enlightened is to understand something - to know.

The rune Cēn does occasionally appear in Old English literature, standing in place of the word 'keen' so we should consider this meaning. Perhaps you need to be bold or brave to express your inner light. How about *cennan*? Some knowledge seems to be brought forth from nowhere, conceived in a moment of inspiration. Should we ignore this?

Today it is difficult to think of this rune as anything other than 'to know/knowledge', but keep your heart open: learning runes is a journey and the meaning you give to the rune needs to be your own and should be the meaning that says yes to you. As we journey through the runes and discover the different aspects of each one, it is as if 'a light goes on'. The information we can recover from within ourselves using research, meditation, thought and experience is ever-growing.

This is a good study rune and taking this rune along on your journey will help you develop your understanding. You may find yourself changing your mind about some of the runes but don't worry your relationship with the English runes should continue to evolve. Keep making notes.

Gyfu - Gift

X

*Gyfu gumena byþ gleng and herenys,
wraþu and wyrþscype and wræcna gehwam
ar and ætwist, ðe byþ oþra leas.*

Gift is an honour and grace of men
a support and adornment, and for any exile
mercy and sustenance when he has no other.

This rune has the phonemic value /g/, as in gate. The rune is pronounced like 'give-oo' but the 'Y' makes an 'i' sound as in ski but with rounded lips; interestingly, you almost kiss the word and it has been long believed that the kisses on a letter or card are in fact this rune. When this 'G' is used in the middle of a word it changes to a 'ch', as in loch, but with a voice sound not an air sound.

This rune seems so simple in today's society: it means a gift and it could be so easy to stop there, but it deserves deeper consideration. A gift to the early English was an exchange that was offered and if you accepted it you were also accepting the responsibility that came with it. As a young man it was a great honour to be offered an arm-ring from your lord, and when you accepted it you knew that you would fight to the death for that lord.

*Gift is of men glory and exaltation,
support and honour, and to every one
honour and sustenance, that hath no other.*
Kemble

If you and your family were hungry, your neighbour would offer you sustenance and you would be expected to give something in return. The favour might not be repaid at that moment, but there would be an unwritten agreement that it would happen at some point. These gifts were given freely: that is, no one was likely to refuse giving them, especially in a time of need, but the understanding was always there; if someone broke the unwritten agreement, they were usually disgraced and forced to leave their tribal group.

To be honest it is similar today. We have the saying 'there is no such thing as a free lunch', and we are often suspicious about offers of free goods and services because they are usually there to entice or catch us into a sale or commitment. Perhaps like many people you think that, as we become more sophisticated, we are increasingly inclined to believe a gift should be free without any implied commitment.

As a society today we often talk about the gift of love and since the 1960s, when the Beatles sang that 'all we need is love', there seems to have been an increased expectation for unconditional love. Unconditional love has its place, but it is a concept for the modern age and perhaps we should be more aware of the relationship between the giver and receiver of the gift. Many people now think giving a gift is a choice and you shouldn't expect anything in return - not even a thank you - but perhaps we are missing a point here. Perhaps we should look to the early English, to whom gift giving was about relationships and about caring and the shared responsibilities of relationships, new and long-standing.

So what does Gyfu mean to you?

We have looked at both of the translations and they mean the same thing. Simply put, it is good and honourable to offer a gift to another person and, for some, receiving that gift may be the lifesaver that they need. Have a think about the gifts you have received during your lifetime: have you always said thank you? What about gifts you have given and not been thanked for - did you feel taken for granted? Make notes in your journal about your feelings, good and bad, concerning this rune. You could experiment with yourself by offering a random act of kindness. How did it make you feel? Perhaps you were thanked, or you received a smile that brightened your day. Did it make you feel good and would you consider this your payback?

How about the gift of love - unconditional love - should we apply this, or tough love? Consider the action of not expecting anything in return: would this devalue your own self-worth? Perhaps expecting your children to be thankful for gifts and to take responsibility for roles within the family will teach them self-worth? This rune is quite simple yet deep, so take time to understand the possible ramifications of a gift.

Wen - Happiness

ᚹ

Wen bruceþ, ðe can weana lyt
sares and sorge and him sylfa hæfþ
blæd and blysse and eac byrga geniht.

Happiness he cannot enjoy who knows little woe
pain and sorrow, and has for himself
wealth and joy, and sufficient protection too.

This rune has the Kentish dialect spelling of the name ascribed to it and the phonemic value /w/ as in window. The rune is pronounced like 'wen' but it can also be spelled wyn or wynn, which changes the pronunciation slightly because the 'Y' makes an 'i' sound with rounded lips.

This rune verse says that 'you can't enjoy happiness if you don't have experience of unhappiness, pain and sorrow, and you can't enjoy it unless you are wealthy, happy and protected. Pollington has translated this as being happiness and in the Elder Futhark this rune is given the meaning of joy, which is sometimes translated as sexual joy; the latter is not obvious in *The Old English Rune Poem*. A look at the meaning of the name given to this rune may be helpful. The *Bosworth-Toller Anglo-Saxon Dictionary* has the meaning of wyn or wynn as:

- *delight, pleasure;*
- *a delight, that which causes pleasure;*
- *the best of a class, the pride of its kind.*

This meaning suggests joy and happiness both physical and emotional but it doesn't explain the fact you can only have it if you have enough money.

> *Hope he needeth not that hath but little want,*
> *soreness and sorrow, and hath himself*
> *increase and bliss and also the enjoyment of borrows.*
> **Kemble**

Kemble translates this rune to be hope and the verse as saying you don't need hope if everything is going well. This certainly relates to human spirituality because our personal spirituality gives us hope. When people experience difficulty in their lives they often look for hope, and people who have never taken part in spiritual rites will look to find a religion or spirituality. If they previously held a spiritual belief they often turn back to it. Unfortunately, religions, hand in hand with state politics, have quite often used hope as an incentive for servitude, preaching that if you work hard and obey the rules in this life you will be rewarded in the next.

Pollington and Kemble have taken the three words at the end of this verse and come to different conclusions. These are the words *'eac byrga geniht'*.

> Eac means, *with, in addition to* and *besides*.
> Byrga has two different meanings: on the one hand it can mean *cities or enclosed dwellings* and on the other it can mean *a surety, bail, a pledger or creditor*.

Although these meanings appear, at first glance, to be entirely different they can both be seen to offer a 'safety net'.

> Geniht means *abundance, fullness and sufficiency*.

Kemble translates this as 'the enjoyment of borrows', which is a way of communicating the ability to borrow whatever is needed. Pollington translates it as 'sufficient protection' - and a city or enclosed dwelling can be seen as sufficient protection.

So what does Wen mean to you?

Have you experienced anyone saying to you 'Wouldn't you like to live in a world where everyone is happy, with no sadness and no pain'? This question can be a real challenge; of course everyone wants to be happy, safe and free of pain and of course this is what we wish for everyone. Why would we consider anything else? This rune verse comes along and tells us that we can't live in a world like this unless we understand its value. It is saying that we can't know happiness unless we know suffering. With this in mind, have a think about the happy things that have happened in your life and also the unhappy things. Use your journal: take a page, draw a line down the middle and make a list of happy occasions in your life on one side and sad occasions on the other side. Have a discussion with a friend about happiness and how to appreciate it. Do you think you can appreciate it without knowing sadness? What about children? All children can be happy even when they have had nothing to cause unhappiness.

Have a look at hope; Kemble suggests you don't need hope if you are not suffering. What do you think? Happiness is something that you can have without money, but what about hope? Think about situations where you could be without hope and how this might be related to money. Today credit is easier to come by and we have insurance and other financial backup. But what if you have no money, no insurance and no ability to borrow? Could you still find hope? Answering these questions can help you to understand this rune and your relationship with it.

Hægl - Hail

ᚻ

*Hægl byþ hwitust corna; hwyrft hit of heofones lyfte,
wealcaþ hit windes scura; weorþeþ hit to wætere syððan.*

Hail is whitest of corn, from heaven's height
it whirls, winds blow it, it becomes water after.

This rune has the phonemic value /h/ as hail. The rune is pronounced 'hail', making sure it sounds like 'hayal'. H has three sounds in old English. One is at the beginning of a word, as in hail. The other two are at the end or in the body of a word: one is like the throaty 'ch' in loch and occurs after a vowel that is pronounced at the back of the mouth, like 'O'; the other one is like the German 'ch' in *ich*, which is more breathy and made further forward in the mouth after a vowel sounding like 'i' as in ski is made at the front of the mouth. It doesn't really need thinking about too much: try going from 'och' to 'ich' and you will find the shape of your mouth changes naturally.

'Hail is the whitest of corn'; this is such a physically descriptive verse, quite beautiful in its description. This is the hail that is most known to the English: it's not too large, it swirls around in the air and then falls, it's over very quickly and it melts almost instantly. This verse seems to describe the type of hail that doesn't really do much harm to crops or property; this hail doesn't appear to knock people unconscious or kill them. Whatever hail the early English experienced - and Bede's Anglo-Saxon chronicles record an incidence of a really bad storm with rain and hail - it could easily have been devastating. The chronicles were created as a written record of Anglo-Saxon history, so it must have been a very bad storm indeed to have been included.

*Hail is whitest of grains, it sweepeth from the lift of heaven.
The showers of wind whirl it about, after it turneth to water.*
Kemble

The Futhorc

Pollington and Kemble translate this verse in agreement with each other. It doesn't appear to be much of a riddle and I think most people who hear the verse will recognise which rune it refers to. Modern-day people, along with the early English, understand the devastation hail can cause, but to the early English the loss of crops would often mean starvation. Hail is more likely to occur during the spring, summer and autumn - the seasons when the crops are in the fields. Although larger hail stones are more likely to form near to mountain ranges, there have been very large hailstones recorded in Britain; one of the largest recorded was the 141-gram Horsham hailstone, which fell on 5th September 1958.

Hail is formed in cumulonimbus clouds, or thunder clouds as they are more commonly known. Thunder does not have a rune of its own but it can be related to hail. Thunder in old English is *Þunor*, a very important god and the early English version of the Norse god Thor. There is not much mention of *Þunor* in the written records of the early English, but his importance is witnessed by many place names such as Thunderley Hall in Essex, Thunderlow in Kent and Thunder's Barrow in Sussex , among many other examples. We also have Thursday, which is said to be Thunorsday or Thorsday, and which corresponds to the Roman day of Jupiter, who was also a thunder god. Although - and probably because - *Þunor* was a very important god to the working people he is, like Woden, not mentioned in text. The original Thor's hammer was actually a club, and miniature clubs have been found in the Rhineland, Germany and also in Anglo-Saxon England.

So what does Hægl mean to you?

With this verse I would encourage you to look at the description well. Is there anything else that could come in looking very attractive and then just melt to nothing? Perhaps there is something devastating that arrives very suddenly and then disappears leaving little trace. Do you have any memories of hail from your childhood? How did you feel about it? Were you excited by the noise and speed of a downfall? Have your feelings changed as you have matured? After you have looked at the obvious meaning of this rune, it is time to meditate on the associated meanings. Do you think this rune could have associations with *Þunor*? When you next experience a storm, watch it carefully; speak to it and ask for inspiration. Have you noticed any patterns to thunderstorms in your area? Where I live we often experience storms out at sea, and sometimes they come inland. When this happens, the storm tracks up one river until it meets a ridge of hills, then follows the ridge until it reaches the next river, where it turns and follows that river down to the sea again. It doesn't happen all of the time, but I have noticed it happening quite often over the years. Once again, write about your thoughts and experiences; this is one rune that deserves returning to after experiencing a hail storm.

Nyd - Need

ᚾ

*Nyd byþ nearu on breostan; weorþeþ hi þeah oft niþa bearnum
to helpe and to hæle gehwæþre, gif hi his hlystaþ æror.*

Need is hard on the heart, yet for men's
sons it often becomes a help and healing if they heed it before.

This rune has the phonemic value /n/ as in need. The rune is pronounced 'need' but because there is a 'Y' in the middle it is pronounced with an 'oo' lip shape.

This is an interesting rune and something of a conundrum. On one hand we can see need; to need something so badly that you can actually feel it in your chest, is something that appears spontaneous. But on the other hand we are being told that need is also a benefit if we are aware of it before it hits us. Once again the translations of Pollington and Kemble have the same meaning, although Kemble's wording is rather different to that which is used now. Kemble talks about need being a narrowing or squeezing of the chest and Pollington advises it is hard on the heart; both describe the deep feeling of need and, in fact, loss: the absence of something.

> *Need is narrow in the breast for the sons of men,
> yet doth it become
> often a help and safety for any one
> if they sooner attend to it.*
> **Kemble**

To try and understand what Nyd meant to the early English we can look, once again at the *Bosworth-Toller Anglo-Saxon Dictionary*. Here we are given several meanings, most of which are very similar. Firstly, the dictionary advises that Nyd is the rune for *níd*, luckily this is only a change in dialect.

Níd means:

- *necessity, inevitability;*
- *need, urgent requirement;*
- *a necessary business, duty,* a matter requiring action to be taken;
- *need, what one wants;*
- *necessity, need, difficulty, hardship, distress;*
- *violence, force, compulsion,* exercised by or upon persons.

This really helps us to understand the second half of the verse because Nyd includes duty, which is something that you are aware of that has to be done. Early English society was full of duty and co-operation; the society functioned on these principles and if you ignored them you would find yourself outside of your community. We have already discussed the responsibility that giving and receiving a gift entails and here we have one of the outcomes. If you receive the gift of an arm ring from your king then it will be your duty to do as he wishes; you understand this when you accept the gift and should be prepared. You would know that one of the duties would be to go into battle when required, and another would be to mete out punishment if required. The definitions include difficulty, hardship and distress, which can be expected if the harvest is not abundant. The early English would prepare for this by keeping, where possible, produce from a previous harvest.

Stephen Pollington in his book *Runes, Literacy in the Germanic Iron Age* suggests that the rune Nyd may be connected to other words in the Germanic language family that mean corpse. It is thought that Nyd may well be the rune that Odin carves to speak with the dead, as described in the *Hávamál'*, verse 158.

A twelfth I know, | if high on a tree
I see a hanged man swing;
So do I write | and colour the runes
That forth he fares,
And to me talks.
Henry Adams Bellows (1885-1939), translation

The Futhorc

So what does Nyd mean to you?

After looking at the verse we can see that the meaning of this rune is likely to be greater than the immediate indication of the heavy feeling in your chest you get when you need or want something so badly it hurts. Today the response to a child when they say 'I need that sweet' is to say 'no, you want that sweet'; this is because most of us believe that need only occurs when you can't survive or function without it. Do you think this still holds true? This rune is often interpreted at face value, using the modern interpretation 'to require (something) because it is essential or very important, rather than just desirable'. This is a perfectly acceptable interpretation of Nyd but it can be so much more. To expand our understanding we should also consider the aspect of duty with this rune. You might like to meditate on this rune to discover what Nyd means in the light of duty and what this was like for the early English. Does the idea of preparing for and understanding a need before it occurs affect your interpretation in any way? Maybe discuss with others what need means to them, and make notes in your journal. Journals can always be re-visited and added to at a later date if you have a sudden flash of inspiration.

Īs - Ice

I

Īs byþ oferceald, ungemetum slidor,
glisnaþ glæshluttur gimmum gelicust,
flor forste geworuht, fæger ansyne.

Ice is too cold and extremely slippery
glass-clear it glistens most like gems
a floor made of frost, fair in appearance.

This rune has the phonemic value /i/, as in is. The rune is pronounced with a long 'i', sounding like 'ee', and the 'S' is a hissing 'ss' not a 'z' sound.

Ice is very cold and very slippery, it glitters like glass, it looks like gemstones and when frost covers large open spaces it is beautiful. Sounds lovely, doesn't it? And just like Hægl, we have something deadly seen in its most beautiful aspect. When we are young we love to go out into the ice and snow: it is a wonder-filled place in which to play, with the chance to build snowmen, create snow angels, throw snowballs, break off an icicle or two and have a sword fight with them. Of course as we get older we become more aware of the dangers; ice can be deadly, the cold kills, and you can slip on the ice and break bones – or worse still, crack your head open. This is a rune that once again gives clues to its name through its beauty, but hides a darker side. Both Pollington's and Kemble's translations agree.

Ice is over-cold, immeasurably slippery;
glittereth bright as glass likest unto gems,
the plain wrought with frost fair to behold.
Kemble

To the early English, ice must have meant danger. Their homes would have been very cold and fire was the only way to keep the ice at bay. The ice always arrived at the dark time of year and very little work could

The Futhorc

be done because even in the daytime the light was low. When the sun or moon shone brightly it would reflect on the ice giving it a beautiful appearance, but this could also be bright enough to hide dangers from sight.

That said, ice is also water; it makes water portable and helps to preserve food. We must not forget that because it is water, ice also flows, although very slowly, and floats. As a seafaring nation, the early English would have encountered icebergs and may also have been aware of glaciers. The *Bosworth-Toller Anglo-Saxon Dictionary* gives us only two meanings: one is ice and the other the rune name, so there is not much more information to be gained there.

The Northern Heathen tradition has a creation myth about how the world was created from fire and ice. Ice was the element that was transformed by fire to create the world. There is no evidence of this myth in the early English writings, but if you look at this myth with a logical view you may be able to see a connection. If you were to stand away from civilisation, somewhere very cold where the snow has fallen and the ice is thick, you would be unlikely to see any signs of life. When the sun gets hotter or you light a fire the ice melts, you may be able to see the ground under the ice and see the beginnings of new life. Today scientists know about the Alaskan wood frog that freezes in the ice but comes back to life when it melts, and there are numerous seeds that need a good frost to germinate. Many early peoples from the northern hemisphere looked upon the bear with great reverence. They looked at its hibernation as a death and its emergence in spring as rebirth. There is proof of many bear cults across all continents in the northern hemisphere; there are many subtle differences in their rites but they tend to centre on the cold, lean time of the year and ultimately associated with human survival.

So what does Īs mean to you?

The word Īs has only one meaning: ice. This indicates everything that goes with this form of water and the environment it creates for us. Consider why the poem only seems to concentrate on the beauty aspect and how slippery it is. Maybe this suggests that the rune indicates something that slips through your fingers. What else can the rune mean to you? Is it another beautiful but deadly thing? Is it something that changes a mundane everyday thing into a beauty to behold?

Do you like gardening? If you do, have you noticed how many seeds need to be planted outside before the winter in order to germinate? It doesn't matter if you don't garden, because a little research into what is called 'cold stratification' and what plants need can broaden your experience of ice and what it means to you. Both fire and ice can be seen as progenitors of new life. Write down your thoughts on this. Perhaps this is also an opportunity to look at the bear cults of the north and to see what clues you can find about indigenous cultures where ice is a serious factor in their yearly life cycle.

Gēr - Harvest

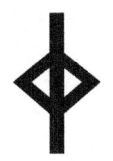

Gēr byþ gumena hiht, ðonne God lætteþ,
halig heofones cyning, hrusan syllan
beorhte bleda beornum ond ðearfum.

Harvest is men's hope when god allows
-holy king of heaven – the earth to give up
fair fruits to warriors and to wretches.

This rune has the phonemic value /j/, which sounds like the 'Y' in you. The rune is pronounced 'y-air', not forgetting to trill the 'R'.

This rune has blatantly Christian wording and this makes it difficult but not impossible to see a pre-Christian explanation. The name of this rune literally means 'year' and the verse describes a good harvest. Once again we have two translations with the same meanings, and if we were sitting in the great hall hearing this verse without knowing the rune name it would definitely indicate harvest. There is evidence that the early English viewed the harvest as the end of the year. The early English lived in a society that relied on agriculture, where bread was the staple part of their diet, and they would have worked hard to gain a successful year's harvest. The result of the harvest would decide which animals lived or died and there were great celebrations when it was good.

The 'Celtic' calendar, according to some, starts at *Calan Gaeaf* (Welsh) or *Samhain* (Irish) when the winter began and the early English calendar appears closer to the modern Western culture by starting just after Christmas. There are many arguments about the start of the year but this is a moot point when you look at what a new year actually is. Today we consider it to be the 1st January but this has only been the case in Britain since 1752, when there was a change from the Julian to the Gregorian calendar. Prior to that new year was the 25th March; for example, the dates would run from the 25th March 1465 to the 24th March 1466, and these dates are in fact the origins of the financial year. There is therefore no reason to discount the idea of a year starting after the grain harvest.

For all early societies the success of the harvest informed all the major decisions such as planning for winter and the planting in spring. Finding out how much fodder there was for the animals helped them decide which ones they could feed over winter. If they had enough grain to feed everyone they had little need to worry about starvation, but if the harvest was poor they needed to decide on rations. It is known that in some very severe cases people would decide that a newborn baby or an elderly relative would not survive the winter and, as dreadful as this may seem today, for the sake of the others they would be left out in the cold to be taken by the gods.

> *Year is the hope of men, when God letteth,*
> *the holy king of heaven, the earth give*
> *her bright increase to rich and poor.*
> **Kemble**

There is another subtle difference between the translations, which concerns Kemble referring to the earth as feminine; this is due to *hrusan*, the earth or ground, being a feminine noun. The early English certainly considered the earth to be feminine and the act of ploughing the earth and planting the seed was an act of procreation. The productivity of the land was and is very important, and to the early English a sheaf of corn was considered very symbolic and holy, as within this symbol is carried the seed of new life as well as the sustenance of bread and ale.

There is a hero called Sceaf in early English writings; the name is Old English for sheaf and he appears in the kings list, i.e. genealogy of King Æðelwulf. There is a story that tells of Sceaf being found in a boat and then growing up to became king. This is similar to the many old stories of babies who have been set adrift and who later became important men. It is thought this could be an analogy of the arrival of grain and agriculture. Another very early god who appears in the early English kings lists is Beow; it's likely that he was originally Proto-Germanic because he is named above/before Woden. He seems to have endured in folk myth and, as *beow* is the old English name for barley, it's possible that he is the origin of John Barleycorn.

The Futhorc

So what does Gēr mean to you?

Look at this rune and its translation both as year and as a measure of time. Do you think you can find this within the rune meaning? Considering harvest and its importance to early peoples can lead to really in-depth studies of the old agrarian celebrations. The early English had one such celebration which continues within pagan celebrations today: *Hlāfmæsse*, which became Lammas and literally means loaf mass or the ritual of the first loaf. Could this rune also hold the meaning of the decisions that need to be made after a failed harvest? How do you think you would cope with having to make similar decisions? Write down your thoughts and feelings about harvest; it is so easy to forget its importance when we can buy anything all year round. What do you know of other celebrations for the harvest, including the harvest festival of the Christian church? There are harvest festivals from all over the world for you to discover, within which you might find deeper meaning to this rune.

Ēoh - Yew

*Ēoh byþ utan unsmeþe treow,
heard hrusan fæst, hyrde fyres,
wyrtrumun underwreþyd, wyn on eþle.*

Yew is an unsmooth tree outside
hard, earthfast, fire's keeper,
underpinned with roots, a joy in the homeland.

This rune has the phonemic value /eː/ and has the sound of a long 'ae', as in aeroplane.

Considering that the yew was such an important tree to the early English, this verse does not seem particularly outstanding. We are told that the outside of the tree is rough and hard, that is it is underpinned with roots that fix it well into the earth. The only other things mentioned are about it being fire's keeper and a joy in the homeland.

*Yew is outwardly an unsmooth tree,
hard, fast in the earth, the shepherd of fire,
twisted beneath with roots, a pleasure on the land.*
Kemble

Both Pollington's and Kemble's translations express the same theme, so let's look at the yew as fire's keeper/shepherd first. Yew wood burns slowly but very well and produces lots of heat. During the long winter nights it was important for the early English to keep warm, and often a fire keeper was needed to ensure that the fire kept up the warmth and didn't go out. It is very possible that yew was specifically kept for burning at night: it burns slowly so would have been less likely to go out, and it burns with a good heat. Using yew at night could mean that the fire didn't need to be tended at all or would enable longer sleep for the fire keeper. If you go onto any bushcraft or survival forum you usually find a section that deals with carrying fire because when you are on the move

The Futhorc

you will need to light a fire at night to keep warm and remain safe from predators. Lighting a fire every night is quite an effort; you either need something to spark a fire or you will have to rub sticks, both of which require energy – and if it is cold this energy would be better used for keeping you warm. One way of lighting a fire very quickly is to carry it with you, and to do this you can carry embers from a yew fire or put embers in a yew container. The yew does not burn away too quickly, allowing you to travel further. Fire has often been carried in bark containers and although it is unlikely that yew bark was used, the wood can be made into boxes.

As we turn our attention to 'a joy in the homeland' we can find other aspects of yew in two other runes: 'Eðel' – homeland or estate, and 'Yr' – yew bow. Bows have been mainly made of yew since the Bronze Age and in order to have the best bows you need yew trees; it is very likely that yew was grown within the estates of the wealthy for this purpose. You will find out more about these other runes later.

One other thing is that the yew is often seen as the World Tree, also known as Yggdrasil, although this is often seen as the ash or the oak depending on which culture you are studying. Yews are evergreen and this made them sacred because the fact that they stay green equates to staying young and alive. The yew also releases the toxin taxine into the air on hot days, which can cause hallucinations. This ability to cause hallucinations is a strong reason to believe that the yew was used for sacred rites. In Norse mythology Odin was gifted, in a vision, with the runes while he was hanging on the World Tree. Yew trees can live for a very long time and were thought of as eternal by early peoples, who often believed that living near them would offer you a longer life; when Christian churches were built this sacred association with the yew tree continued. Today the oldest yews are often found in churchyards, indicating the eternal life gained by following the Christian path.

So what does Ēoh mean to you?

You can see above that this rune can mean more than just a rough-looking tree. Is there anything else that you can find out about the yew tree? The yew is a very good tree to sit and talk with. If you can find a yew tree locally, for example in a churchyard, you can make friends with it. Sit peacefully with it, close your eyes and ask for a vision about this rune. Penny Billington's book is a very good source of ways in which a connection with these trees can be obtained, and includes insights into her own experience with yews. If you are lucky enough to find a yew wood or forest, take time to walk through it; if you can find a mother tree, take a look at the bark and the branches. Don't forget your journal.

Peorð – Gaming

*Peorð byþ symble plega and hlehter
wlancum [on middum], ðar wigan sittaþ
on beorsele bliþe ætsomne.*

Gaming is always play and laughter
to proud men... where warriors sit
in the beerhall happily together.

This rune has the phonemic value /p/, as in papa. The rune name uses the diphthong 'eo' found in 'eoh', with a trilled 'R' followed by 'th'.

Pollington's translation indicates gaming as the meaning of the rune and this verse reflects the mood of the early English feast hall along with its place in society. Feasting was important for everyone and especially for warriors before battle. Playing games of chance, feasting and having fun in the feast hall, or 'beer cellar' (*beorsele*) as it is called in this verse, is important because every day must be lived to the full and it might be the last time that companions are together, at least in this life. In the verse, they have taken part in Symbel – the ritual held as the first part of every feast, which involved the giving and receiving of loyalties, promises, toasts and boasts – and now they are having fun. The early English seemed to do substantial amounts of lot-casting and gambling: winning was very important to them.

There is no written evidence of an early English Valhalla but there is reference to the *Wælcyrigean*, Old English for Valkyrie. Due to the importance of the feast hall and the ritual of Symbel, which has close connections to bravery and battle, it is very likely that any belief the early English had in an afterlife would include a large feasting hall.

> *Chessman is ever play and laughter*
> *to the proud, where warriors sit*
> *in the beer-hall blithe together.*
> Kemble

Kemble's idea of chessman is another deduction from the poem. There is no real translation for the word Peorð, as it appears only in the Elder Futhark and the Anglo-Frisian Rune Row; the only clues to the rune name and meaning appear in *The Old English Rune Poem*. Gaming can be seen as a better translation: using games of luck like rolling dice. Chess appears more cerebral and the outcome is influenced by skill, which is great for learning strategy and holding your nerve but I am certain that less laughter would be involved.

The written word Peorð is not found anywhere else in surviving Old English works and no one has found a convincing meaning for it; I have even seen the meaning of 'a pear tree' associated with this rune. However, Peorð seems very close to the Welsh word *porth*, which means a gate, a door, the mouth of a river or a portal. These are boundary openings and all boundaries are liminal places: a portal gives access from one side to the other, and at the roll of a dice you could find yourself on either side. Expanding on this idea connects this rune with liminal places and the guidance or danger to be found in them. Maybe there is the chance of meeting and speaking with the ancestors or the potential danger of other unseen creatures such as the *Wiht* or Wights.

So what does Peorð mean to you?

This is a complex rune due to the ambiguity of its name. It is clear though that it is associated with the feast hall, games of chance and laughter. Does this word remind you of anything? What about its shape? Lying down on its back Peorð looks like a dice-throwing vessel or perhaps a cauldron. It is one rune where you can freely meditate unrestrained to discover what it means to you: it is a rune of possibilities. Make an effort to engage in the same sort of activity as described in the poem, such as going to a celebratory feast or party - it could be a get-together with friends who have watched the same match or visit the local pub or sports bar on a match night. Notice how elated they feel if they are on the winning side, how they replay parts of the match back and discuss tactics. Can you feel the camaraderie? Perhaps you can visit a casino to watch people throwing dice and playing cards, or hold a games night at home with friends. These experiences will give you a glimpse into the atmosphere of the feast hall and how luck can change from good to bad in the blink of an eye.

There is a suggestion from this verse that life can change at the throw of a dice, and lot-casting is considered as a method for discovering the paths of Wyrd. How about visiting liminal places, such as the wet part of the seashore when the tide is out, and asking the ancestors for their help and guidance? Whatever conclusions you come to make sure you write them down in your journal.

Eolhx - Elk

ᛉ

*Eolhx-secg eard hæfþ oftust on fenne
wexeð on wature, wundaþ grimme,
blode breneð beorna gehwylcne
ðe him ænigne onfeng gedeþ.*

Elk-grass most often dwells in a fen,
grows in water, harshly wounds
marks with blood any warrior
who tries to take it.

This rune has the phonemic value /ks/, like kiss without the 'i', or it may be /xs/ which is like the 'ck in lock + 's'. The rune name is pronounced 'eo-l-ks or eo-l-ks-edge'.

Eolhx as a letter sound in early English is very difficult to find, as it was rarely used except to replace the Latin letter chi (x) in literature. An example can be seen on St Cuthbert's Coffin, 698 CE, where runes are used for the Christogram *ihs xps* and Eolhx is used in place of the Greek letter chi.

The verse is very simple and it seems likely to be describing a type of sedge or grass as both translations suggests. Many sedges have razor-sharp edges, especially ones in the *Carex* genus, which are known as true sedges and would have been growing in England at the time of *The Old English Rune Poem*. They can cut you badly if you grab hold of them and pull, and they grow in marshy places.

This rune requires a look at the earliest source we have for the poem, George Hickes' facsimile, where we find that the word written for the name of the rune is Eolhx. Many translations call the rune Eolhx-secg and the only use of Eolhx-secg is in translations of the rune poem, so this is an assumption. The sedge part of the translation comes from a word that

The Futhorc

is written *seccard* in the Hickes document and is assumed to be a miscopy of two words: *sec eard*. Although there is no word 'sec' in Old English literature, with the rest of the verse in mind it is difficult to see any word other than sedge as the translation.

> *Sedge hath dwelling oftest in the fen,*
> *waxeth in water, grimly woundeth,*
> *burneth in the blood, every man*
> *that any way toucheth it.*
> Kemble

The placing of secg is within the verse and so shows it is not the name of the rune that is called Eolhx. The verse talks about sedge, a rather nasty plant growing in the fen, and this should be suggesting the actual name of the rune. The word Eolhx was originally Eolh, which means elk. The Eurasian elk, sometimes known as a moose, is related to the American moose. The 'X' has been added for the purpose of changing its letter sound, which was 'Z' from the proto Germanic word *Algiz*, while the 'Z' was already covered by the use of 'S'. So in the *OERP* we have an 'X' that would only really used by scribes of Latin in exchange for a 'Z', which was no longer needed. This suggests that this rune needed to be preserved, and with its original meaning of elk. The Latin name for the Eurasian elk is *alces, alces* and it is believed that *alces* is a Latin word derived from the proto-Germanic word *Algiz*. The conclusion that sedge is part of the verse does not discount the idea that there was a plant known as elk sedge, it just strengthens the suggestion that the rune name is Eolhx.

The Eurasian elk, *alces, alces*, is a very large animal; it was comparable in size and behaviour to the Aurochs and was known to roam in a similar way. There are still survivors today and they can be found in Scandinavia, Poland, Czechoslovakia, Russia and China, but their numbers are much lower now. They love to live in marshland and, as they are very good swimmers, they can be found diving for underwater vegetation. They are also known to attack humans if startled or mishandled, and the females will attack to protect their young. It is very likely that the early English warriors would test their skills against an elk. This verse can be as true of the elk as it is of sedge: it likes to live on marshy land, it grows higher or bigger in water, where it finds its food, and it would wound any warrior who tried to fight it or capture it.

There is another aspect to the Eurasian elk that seems to have a connection to the Alcis, divine twins, mentioned by Cornelius Tacitus in his 1st century work Germania.

> *The Naharvali proudly point out a grove associated with an ancient worship. The presiding priest dresses like a woman; but the deities are said to be the counterpart of our Castor and Pollux. This indicates their character, but their name is the Alcis. There are no images, and nothing to suggest that the cult is of foreign origin; but they are certainly worshiped as young men and as brothers.* Cornelius Tacitus, Germania

Although there is no indication here of what the Alcis look like, the name is clearly linked to *Algiz* and the Proto-Indo-European word **h1elkis*. The interesting thing about Eurasian elk is that they often give birth to twins – something that is unusual for such a large mammal. Divine twins are sometimes found with one human and one animal twin and in this case I am reminded of the Cernunnos plate on the Gundestrup Cauldron, which depicts a human form with antlers next to an antlered beast. Due to the Alcis connection the rune is often connected with protection in the sense of the protection and safety found in a sacred grove.

So what does Eolhx mean to you?

Once again we have a complex rune due to the ambiguity of its name, but this time it is perhaps due to misspelling. Hickes' copy was read and an early academic decision was made that the rune name should include the first word in the verse. Do you think this may be due to a lack of information about the Eurasian elk at the time of earlier translation? As with all the runes it is up to you to decide the meaning. The information above is not comprehensive and you can find out about the different aspects of this rune with further research. Once again, meditation after research is extremely helpful, but don't forget that lightning strike of inspiration – don't ignore this, and write any thoughts down, however strange. You will be able to decide later if you want to keep an idea or lose it.

Sigel - Sun

Sigel semannum symble biþ on hihte,
Ðonne hi hine feriaþ ofer fisces beþ,
oþ hi brimhengest bringeþ to lande.

Sun to seamen is always a hope
when they travel over the fish's bath
until the sea-steed brings them to land.

This rune has the phonemic value /s/, as in sun. The rune name is pronounced 'see-gh-el'; the 'gh' has the sound of a voiced 'ch': it is a very soft 'g' sound and has the phonemic value of /ɣ/.

The verse for this rune is fairly uncomplicated: the sun gives sailors constant hope as they travel over the sea, right until their boat reaches land. The early people of the world learned to travel over water as it was easier to travel around the coasts and up rivers than to traverse the uneven, dangerous, unknown inland terrain. Early habitation patterns are found on coastal and riverbank areas where food was plentiful and transportation in boats was fairly easy. The early English were a seafaring nation; the Angles, Saxons and Jutes arrived by boat in the migration period during the 5th century CE and, according to Caesar, there were already people of Belgic descent living in southern Britain and travelling back and forth to see family on the European mainland.

Most travel on the sea required the sailors to keep within sight of the land and so it was undertaken during daylight hours, which also meant most travel was planned for the summer months when the sun was in the sky for longer. There were many reasons for the presence of the sun being a positive occurrence for early English sailors, such as the fact that they could of course see the coast and any other familiar markers for navigation, or that if there was sun with no cloud it was likely to be fairly smooth out at sea. All sailors know how the sea can change: you set sail in good weather and then the winds pick up and storm clouds roll in, and it is very unlikely that the sun will be present in the midst of a storm.

> *Sail to seamen is always confidence,*
> *when they bear it over the fishes bath,*
> *till them the sea horse bringeth to land.*
> Kemble

Kemble believed that there was a misspelling and that Sigel should have been Segel, which means sail; this fits well with the verse and seems to make a good case for this idea. There has been argument over the years on whether the Anglo-Saxon ships had sails. They had oars and many archaeologists have said that the lack of a deep keel and proper mast supports means there were no sails. Although this argument has not yet been settled in the field and no ships have been found from the Anglo-Saxon era that are considered fit for sails by many academics, the world of experimental archaeology has other experience to offer.

A half-size boat reconstructed from the Sutton Hoo ship and called the *Sae Wylfing* was built and sailed in 1993 by Edwin and Joyce Gifford. The *Sae Wylfing* was used in many different weather conditions, including high waves, and the hull was capable of holding the sail steady without breaking the boat up; this proved to the Giffords that the early English knew about building and sailing ships. The Romans had sailing ships before the Anglo-Saxon era and it is very likely that there were sailing ships around the Rhine area in Germany. Even if the people living near the Rhine hadn't had sails prior to that time, they would have started to develop the technology. Furthermore, we know that the early English had extended family in those areas.

Another Old English word for the sun is *Sunne*, which is a feminine noun. It is possible that both the sun and moon – *Mona* in OE and a masculine noun – were both worshipped, their importance remaining today in the naming of Sunday and Monday. This may be a riddled meaning for this rune.

So what does Sigel mean to you?

Whatever the rune was called, the verse is translated in the same way by both Pollington and Kemble, which shows that the meaning behind the rune is the same. What do you think – sun or sail? The decision is totally up to you and it may be that you include both, depending on the situation behind its use. We know the early English moved back and forth across the waters to mainland Europe before Caesar's visit to Britain in 54 BCE, and it is highly likely that they used sails. What about the sun and how this might assist those early sailors? What qualities do you think are associated with this rune regarding the sun and how it helped early sailors? They didn't have any of the navigation equipment we have today, so if you are interested in the type of clues that helped early sea travellers then I recommend Tristan Gooley's book *How to Read Water: Clues, Signs & Patterns from Puddles to the Sea*. Tristan's speciality is natural navigations in all environments.

With *Sunne* being another name for sun and likely a deity worshipped by the early English, do you think that the name of the rune may be this? What do you think of the sun being a feminine deity? Does this affect how you view this rune? Reread the verse and note how you feel about the importance of the sun deity to sailors. Once again, note your thoughts and feelings in your journal.

Tīr – Tiw (a god)

↑

*Tīr biþ tacna sum, healdeð trywa wel
wiþ þelingas; a biþ on færylde
ofer nihta genipu, næfre swiceþ.*

Tiw is one of the signs, holds faith well
with noblemen, on a journey is always
Above the night's gloom, never fails.

This rune has the phonemic value /t/, as in tell. The rune name is pronounced 'tīr' with a long 'i' sound, much like saying 'tea-r' with a trilled 'R'.

This rune, although named Tīr in MS Cotton Ortho B. x. fol. 165 , is thought to mean the god Tiw or Tiwaz/Teiwaz, who the Romans equated to Mars, god of war; but the name Tiw is related to Zeus, and Jupiter the sky father. In Old Norse this god is called *Tyr*, in Old English *Tiw*, Old High German *Ziu*, and the name is derived from the Indo-European *Dyeus*. The god name Tiwaz appears as a god of the sun and of judgement, which can be traced back to the Luwian-language speakers associated with the Hittites of Anatolia, 1,600 BCE to 1,180 BCE. He was depicted bearing a winged sun on his crown or headdress, and a crooked staff.

Tacitus reports how punishment in early Germanic society was not decided by the people's leaders; this right was only permitted to the priests of their god of war, Tiw, and as such it was the god's judgement alone. The following account by Tacitus demonstrates the aspect of Tiw that ties him to judgement:

> *They choose their kings by birth, their generals for merit. These kings have not unlimited or arbitrary power, and the generals do more by example than by authority. If they are energetic, if they are conspicuous, if they fight in the front, they lead because they are admired. But to reprimand, to imprison, even to flog, is*

The Futhorc

permitted to the priests alone, and that not as a punishment, or at the general's bidding, but, as it were, by the mandate of the god whom they believe to inspire the warrior.
Cornelius Tacitus, Germania

Tiw appears to be an early god from pre-English times and it is very difficult to find any information about him in early English Literature. We do however have his name preserved as Tuesday and in a few place names including Tuesley in Surrey, Tysoe in Warwickshire and Tyesmere in Worcester. We also know that this rune was inscribed on weapons and cremation urns. There is evidence that Tir/Tiw may also be represented by the Pole Star and therefore part of the constellation Ursa Minor; it's position can also be found via Ursa Major, known as the plough or big dipper.

Tir is a token; it holdeth confidence well
with nobles: ever it is moving
over the darkness of night: never it resteth.
Kemble

Pollington and Kemble both agree how the verse is translated and seems to be about two things: a sign that holds faith and a star, constellation or sign in the night sky that never fails. The word *tir* in Old English translates as glory and we know that the Tīr rune was used extensively on weapons as the victory rune. It is thought that its use on weapons gave a certain protection while helping the warrior with courage and valour. Holding a weapon dedicated to glory/victory and blessed by the god of war would set any warrior up for the challenge of battle. We know from Tacitus that the Germanic god of war was also a god of judgement, so we can conclude that Tir/Tiw would also decide if the warrior was to live or die and that the outcome was his judgement alone.

As for cremation urns, no one really knows why this rune appears so often: as it isn't just on the urns of warriors, perhaps this is related to protection going back in time to when Tiw was the sky father and protector. It could also relate to the judgement aspect and a sign of respect that will hopefully offer a good afterlife.

Tir/Tiw in the night sky is thought by many to be the Pole Star and Pollington's translation allows for this as he translates it as 'always being there as a constant for journeys'. However, Kemble translates the verse as Tir being 'ever moving over the darkness'. Once again both translations are correct; Old English is a complex language and the early English loved their riddles, both of which can make it very difficult to be precise.

So what does Tīr mean to you?

This rune was obviously extremely important to the early English and we can plainly see this in its use on weapons and cremation urns. As I have mentioned before, the rune names come from Hickes' manuscript and these rune names were not originally part of the poem, as they were added later – although no one knows exactly when. How do you think this rune will work for you? When do you feel would be the best use of its influence? Make a list of the influences that this rune may have and list them in your journal; it may be that reading more on the Indo-European sky gods will help you. What do you think of Tiw as the Pole Star? Do you think there is a particular star or constellation that you want to associate with this rune? It is also up to you to decide whether to call this rune Tīr or Tiw: either is perfectly acceptable.

Beorc - Birch

Beorc byþ bleda leas, bereþ efne swa ðeah
tanas butan tudder, biþ on telgum wlitig,
heah on helme hrysted fægere,
geloden leafum, lyfte getenge.

Birch is fruitless, yet bears
shoots without seeds, is pretty in its branches
high in its spread, fair adorned
laden with leaves, touching the sky.

This rune has the phonemic value /b/, as in birch. The rune name is pronounced either 'bay-ork' or 'bay-orch'. I have separated the vowel sounds with a hyphen, but you should try and smooth it all together.

Let us look at this verse, both translations agree with each other, it starts by telling us that this tree is fruitless and we know that the birch tree bears catkins. It's possible, as many scholars believe, that the verse may have originally described another tree, but no one knows which one. It could be the white poplar, which is found in mainland Europe, or the aspen, which is native to Britain – both will spread readily using root suckers. Aspens like to grow into large colonies, spreading in this manner due to their seeds needing good sunlight; it is better for them to multiply using suckers as the seeds don't tend to flourish in wooded areas. Both the white poplar and the aspen have catkins that spread seeds, and the birch tree also has the ability to spread using root suckers. All of these trees are pretty, tall and laden with lovely leaves that seem to touch the sky.

Birch is fruitless; Nevertheless it beareth
twigs without increase; it is beautiful in its branches;
still it is at top fairly adorned,
laden with leaves, heavy in the air.
Kemble

Of the trees mentioned above it is the birch that is most associated with myth, folklore and ancient history. The root of its name can be traced back to the Indo-European language: birch paper has a Sanskrit name and it was used for ancient Indian texts. Birch bark becomes loose and can be peeled off in fine sheets and used for writing even today. Also, birch sap, which can be taken from the tree when the sap first starts to rise in spring, may be used as a sugar substitute, and wine and beer are often made from it. Birch bark is a very durable material full of oils that prevent it from decomposing which make it waterproof: many items, from canoes to water carriers, are made from birch bark. The birch is also one of the first things to look for when lighting a fire: it burns easily from a spark and the wood burns when wet.

The birch tree has many spiritual connections. They are one of the pioneer trees that start to populate barren land and as such they are connected to new beginnings and growth. The birch is also one of the first trees to leaf in spring and therefore is closely associated with spring rites. In Europe its branches are often brought into people's houses to chase away the winter and is associated with spring goddesses throughout Europe and beyond. The birch is important in both Welsh and Irish folklore and is the first tree in the Ogham alphabet. There is far too much information about the birch tree to mention here, but a little research on its plant nature and its practical and spiritual associations will offer great rewards.

So what does Beorc mean to you?

Looking at the verse yourself, what do you think about the name? Could it still be birch even though the birch tree bears fruit? One way to find out is to visit a birch tree and sit with it for a while. Have a conversation with the tree; it may take a while, because although they are full of wisdom, they live in a slower-paced world than we do. If you find you enjoy connecting with trees or wish to make deeper connections, then as mentioned before there is Penny Billington's brilliant book, *The Wisdom of Birch, Oak and Yew*; the section on birch will really help inform your understanding of this rune. If you are of a practical nature, one way to get close to this tree is to make something from the wood or bark. If you are lucky enough to find a supplier you could always sit quietly and contemplate while sipping a nice cool glass of birch wine.

Eh – Horse

ᛖ

Eh byþ for eorlum æþelinga wyn,
hors hofum wlanc, ðær him hæleþ ymb[e]
welege on wicgum wrixlaþ spræce
and biþ unstyllum æfre frofur.

Steed is noblemen's joy before heroes,
a hoof-proud horse where about it warriors
rich in stallions exchange words
and is always a comfort to the restless.

This rune has the phonemic value of /e/, as in energy, and the rune is pronounced 'e-h'. The Old English language is phonetic and pronounces all the letters in a word.

The name given to this rune is usually 'horse', and to the early English a horse was very valuable. But the poem suggests more; it suggests that this is actually a steed most valued by noblemen. Pollington gives the name Steed, Old English *steda* meaning stallion, and very likely an especially spirited, brave stallion. Nobles and warriors would boast about how brave and fast their horses were and of course their own horse would be the best for some amazing reason, in much the same way as people boast about their cars today. After all, if you have a swift and reliable mode of transport, you can go anywhere.

As a comfort to the restless; we can see that a horse, even one of lesser quality, was important to everyone in early English society. You can find many references to horses in the Old English manuscripts: carthorses, packhorses, riding horses, horses for breeding, horses for royalty, and warhorses. With a horse it is easier to move from place to place when you need to.

Horse is for men the joy of nobles,
Steed proud of hoofs where the heroes
Wealthy on their horses interchange speech:
And to the restless it is ever a comfort.
Kemble

Horses were very important in early society and England has the White Horse of Uffington standing proudly on the hillside. It is the oldest of our chalk carvings (1200-800 BCE) and is placed very close to the Ridgeway, an ancient trackway with one end in Avebury, Wiltshire and the other at Ivinghoe Beacon, Buckinghamshire. There have been archaeological finds of early harness parts along the Ridgeway and also finds around England of horse burials, where the horse with bridle and saddle was buried with a human.

The ability to domesticate the horse is one of the most important discoveries of early human society and is thought to have happened around 3500 BCE. Along with other animals, horses were used, at first, to pull wheeled vehicles like chariots, carts and wagons. Later they were increasingly used for riding, becoming high-status animals of great importance and prestige. They were even venerated, as we can see with the British goddess Rhiannon and with the Gaulish goddess Epona: the Gauls believed that Epona and her horses transported the soul into the afterlife. In early English society this can be seen as related to the horses of Woden's Wild Hunt.

Bede in his *Historia Ecclesiastica Gentis Anglorum* (*The Ecclesiastical History of the English People*) tells us about Hengist and Horsa, two brothers who led the invading armies that first conquered Britain in the 5th century CE. The names Hengist and Horsa are Old English words for stallion and horse and there is reason to believe that they were in fact horse deities and divine twins. Bede's history is not always clear on some aspects, so instead of being the invaders perhaps they were the deities of the invaders. Hengist and Horsa are found in the ancestral king lists for Kent.

So what does Eh mean to you?

On the surface this is one of the clearer verses, but if you dig deeper it can lead you on a journey of exploration into the world and mythology of the horse, and could deepen the meaning for you. This verse talks about a personal belonging, something valued very highly that is a comfort when you feel restless. It is something you can boast about with your friends and neighbours. Do you have anything like this? It could be your car or your bike. Have you observed this behaviour in yourself or others? Do you ever feel restless, with a hankering to visit places you have never been to? How do you think this rune relates to this feeling? Hopefully you are keeping up with your journal, so have a think about it and make notes on your observations.

Man - Mankind

Man byþ on myrgþe his magan leof:
sceal þeah anra gehwylc oðrum swican,
forðum drihten wyle dome sine
þæt earme flæsc eorþan betæcan.

Man is dear to his kinsmen in mirth
yet each one must fail the others
since by his judgement the lord wishes
to commit the poor flesh to earth.

This rune has the phonemic value of /m/, as in man, and the rune is pronounced 'man' with the 'A' being pronounced somewhere between the sound of 'ah' and 'oar'.

Man in Old English means mankind and not a male human. This verse really seems to be a statement that 'we are loved by our family and friends and this brings great joy and happiness, but unfortunately we will die and leave them behind in grief'. It may be that we die and leave our families in debt, something we can resolve with planning today but which wasn't so easy back in the days of the early English. Both translations agree and the verse may either relate to Christian judgement and burial or to the earlier tribal lords and a belief in which bodies were cremated. The early English used both burial and cremation in pagan and Christian times. The translation of this rune as mankind is important though because some, often esoteric interpretations, of the *OERP* tend to consider it as male oriented and then go out of their way to bring the female aspects when in fact early English society was pretty well balanced.

The Futhorc

Man is in mirth dear to his kindred;
and yet must every one depart from other,
because the Lord will by his doom
the wretched flesh commit to earth.
Kemble

Essentially this rune appears to be about mankind, both as human individuals and as part of a larger social group. Humans are naturally social animals and in early history we lived together in smaller groups based on family ties; when those groups got too large, there was often a split with part of the group leaving to find another area to live. Human society consists of different types of characters that fit in with this small-group pattern: there is perhaps an alpha male who becomes the leader, then there are those who like to advise and those who are happy to work hard to feed the community; there are also entertainers, travellers and all sorts of other characters who create a whole. Sometimes a male challenger appears, perhaps as the younger males grow up, and then there is a contest to see who should lead. This is a simplistic view, but we can see that this behaviour is reflected throughout the animal world. We are all essentially animal and this was recognised by the early English whose tribal groups were often associated with animals. These animals were thought of as role models or even as ancestors. This model of society was a closer reality for the early English who essentially lived in smaller groups, but also, later, as part of larger groups being formed under kings. The larger the group the more laws were required to ensure the safety and wellbeing of everyone and to prevent would-be kings trying to take over.

Today many of us have lost touch with our place in the world, our place in nature; we assume that we are superior to all other life forms and therefore somehow better. There have been debates during Christian history about whether animals have souls like us; Saint Thomas Aquinas (1225-74) argued that only humans have an immortal soul indicating the progression of human superiority. It could though have been because animals wouldn't obey the laws.

So what does Man mean to you?

Mankind is amazing and unique, but do you think we are better than other forms of life? Think about your attitude to your place in the world, your moral compass. Consider how mankind fits in with the animistic view. How does this view fit in with the food chain? Mankind is very high up in the food chain and in Britain we have destroyed all the animals that could have been considered equal or higher.

Considering animals as ancestors fits in with an animistic belief system and in an animistic society everything has an equal right to its life: humans, animals, rocks, rivers, the sky, thunder and even items that have been made by man are considered to have a spirit and soul. Do you find yourself talking to inanimate items and giving them names? Many people experience a change in the behaviour of, perhaps a washing machine, when they talk to it and treat it with respect. Have you done this?

The verse talks about failing or departing from each other. Have you suffered the loss of someone you love? Did you feel angry because they left you? Did you feel guilty for feeling that way? It is now understood that animals share this grief, especially when a life partner dies. Have you experienced or heard about this? Make notes about your feelings and also observe how others think and behave. The more you understand about yourself, and the more you learn about mankind and our place in the world, the more you will understand this rune.

Lagu - Water (Large body of)

Lagu byþ leodum langsum geþuht,
gif hi sculun neþan on nacan tealtum
and hi sæyþa swyþe bregaþ
and se brimhengest bridles ne gym[eð].

Water is seemingly endless to men
if they must fare on a tilting ship
and sea-waves frighten them mightily
and the sea-steed does not heed the bridle.

This rune has the phonemic value of /l/, as in lake. The rune is pronounced 'la' with the 'a' sound somewhere between the sound of 'ah' and 'oar', and then the 'gu' sounds like goo; however, the 'G' is soft /ɤ/ because in the middle of the word it changes to a 'ch', as in loch, but with a voice sound not an air sound.

The translations by Pollington and Kemble are in agreement: travelling over water seems to take forever, especially when it is rough and the ship wants to do its own thing.

> *Water to men seemeth tedious,*
> *if they must venture on the unsteady boat,*
> *and the sea waves heavily whirl them,*
> *and the sea stallion heed not the bridle.*
> **Kemble**

The verse communicates that this is a large body of water because it seems endless, especially when it is rough; such large bodies of water include oceans as well as large lakes, which can get pretty turbulent in bad weather too. Water connects us all via the oceans: one ocean becomes another ocean connected to yet another, until the whole world is joined together - and people seem to have travelled over water from earliest times. Water brings people together in trade and communication as well as being the home of the fish that people have eaten for millennia. Water deserves respect: many have lost their lives at sea catching fish for our tables, and water seems to play by its own rules.

Our bodies are mostly water, and it is the largest component in all warm-blooded and cold-blooded animals; it is also a large part of all plant life. Without water the planet would die. We connect water with the moon through the tides and if you live near the shore or go fishing you are likely to watch the moon closely. It is even said that the moon exerts influence over the water in our bodies, changing our moods and behaviour. You can see this relationship expressed in the word 'lunatic', which originally referred to epilepsy and madness caused by the moon, and many nurses will agree that patients become less settled and often unruly during a full moon.

A quick look at the *Bosworth-Toller Anglo-Saxon Dictionary* gives us two definitions for this rune name.

> Lagu:
> *sea, water*
> *law, statute, decree, regulation, rule, fixed custom*

We know the early English loved their riddles, so this rune could be related to the law. Law seems tedious, especially if you want adventure and excitement, but if you break the law and get caught you can find it ends in a rough ride. This of course is not a literal translation, but it is in the spirit of the verse.

It is established that the word this verse refers to is Lagu as water because this is the obvious thought on hearing or reading it, but we can't ignore the other meaning of Lagu. The oldest written English laws codes were derived from spoken law and were written down into 'law code' by King Æthelberht of Kent. These laws were very similar in nature to the law codes of our closest neighbours across the water. It is thought by some that Roman influence in Europe brought law to our shores. The laws of the early English were actually not greatly influenced by Rome and when law was written down it was in Old English and not Latin. The Church did have an influence on law as it had its own laws, but these did not increase in influence until the early English kings were Christianised. For the early English, law would have grown out of nature and community with legislation becoming stronger and rulers having tighter controls as their communities grew from tribal communities into kingdoms, and then to states, and then to a union.

So what does Lagu mean to you?

Most people from pagan, heathen or occult belief systems automatically connect water with emotion. Do you feel the same? Can you connect emotion to the verse? Think about the different natures of water. If you have access to the sea, make a point of visiting every week. Try to visit in different types of weather. What differences do you see? How does the effect of the weather make you feel?

Think about the law and how it is used in society. Think about different words used in seafaring and law. You could put two columns in your journal, one for water and the other for law, and list the descriptive words for each to see if there are words that are common to both. Do you think law should also be considered for this rune? This rune seems to offer very little when you first read the verse, but it expands beautifully the more you look into it.

Ing - Ing (a god, thought to be Frea)

*Ing wæs ærest mid east-denum
gesewen secgun, oþ he siððan est
ofer wæg gewat; wæn æfter ran;
ðus Heardingas ðone hæle nemdun.*

Ing was first among the East Danes
seen by men until he later eastwards
went across the waves, the waggon sped behind,
Thus the hard men named the hero.

This rune has the phonemic value of /ŋ/, as in the 'ng' in song. The rune is pronounced 'ing' just like the end of words such as 'jumping', 'shopping', and so on. The 'G' on the end is sometimes pronounced: we can hear 'ing' being pronounced differently around the English-speaking world, so it was probably the same for the early English, but the best way is to pronounce it more as a stop or with a very slight, light non-voiced 'g'.

Ing is a name that is little known, and Ing as a hero is unknown in Old English texts other than *The Old English Rune Poem* (*OERP*) in Hickes' manuscript. Ing is an Old English is patronymic - referring to 'children of' or 'kin of' - and can be seen in Steyning, Lancing and many other village names in the south-east of Britain.

*Ing was first among the East Danes
seen by men; till he afterwards again
departed over the wave; his chariot ran behind him.
Thus the warriors named the man.*
Kemble

The verse tell us that Ing was of the East Danes, that he was connected with a wagon which went across the waves, and that he was a hero of the Heardingas. From this we can surmise that Ing was possibly an early

The Futhorc

god/hero from across the water and in his writings on Germania, Tacitus talks about the Ingvaeones, or Ingwine (the friends of Ing) in Old English. The Ingwine are mentioned in *Beowulf*, where Hrothgar of the Danes is referred to as their protector or lord. The Ingvaeones came from the area that includes modern Denmark, ancient Frisia and the low countries of the Netherlands and Belgium.

Ing or Ingwe in Old English is thought to be a fertility god due to his association with the wagon or cart; his name comes from the same root as *Inguin* in Old High German and *Yngvi* in Old Norse, and the Proto-Germanic name is Ingwaz. It is likely that Ing was given the title Frea, which means 'lord'. Stephen Pollington talks about Frea in his book *The Elder Gods, The Other World of Early England*, where he tells of the use of the name Frea in the oldest surviving verse 'Caedmon's Hymn'. The version of 'Caedmon's Hymn' mentioned is specifically the Old Northumbrian version and suggests that when you look closely, the poem could equate to a heathen creation myth. Caedmon is known to have used his knowledge of older traditional material to make the conversion to Christianity less onerous. Caedmon's Hymn appears to tell how the sky father or heaven's keeper created the heavens, and then the earth and earth's keeper, the almighty Frea. The use of the title 'Frea' once again connects Ing with the Old Norse *Yngvi*, known as *Yngvifreyr* or *frea inguin* in Old English. In later Norse stories, Frea is drawn in a cart or wagon to bless the fields.

There was a wagon cult stretching back to the Bronze Age, possibly even further, with images of wagons found across northern Europe on stone and in statues, so many of them that it must have been of huge importance. Cornelius Tacitus observed the following:

> *The Lombardi are distinguished by their common worship of Nerthus, Mother Earth, and believe that she is interested in the affairs of humans and rides among the people. There is a sacred grove on an island in the Ocean, in which there is a consecrated chariot, draped with cloth, where the priest alone may touch. He perceives the presence of the goddess in the innermost shrine and with great reverence escorts her in her chariot, which is drawn by female cattle. There are days of rejoicing then and the countryside celebrates the festival, wherever she decides to visit and to accept hospitality. No one goes to war, no one takes up arms, all objects of iron are locked away, then and only then do they experience peace and quiet. This continues until the goddess*

has had her fill of human company and the priest brings her back to her temple. Afterwards the chariot, the cloth, and, if one may believe it, the Goddess herself are washed in a hidden lake. The slaves who perform this rite are immediately drowned in the same lake. Cornelius Tacitus, Germania

The insistence on the removal of iron in any form, but especially weapons, indicates that this was, as suggested, a pre-Iron Age cult. The celebrations would have been times of great joy and love-making to enhance the fertility of the land.

Other than the aforementioned verse in the *OERP* and the use of 'ing' as a patronymic, or as a word for field in the north of England (probably a fertile one), it is nearly impossible to find any trace of Ing and the wagon cult in Britain, except perhaps in Sussex. There is a story about St Cuthmann of Steyning who after the death of his father pulled his mother, in a cart, eastward towards the rising sun. He created a halter for himself and decided to pull the cart with his mother in it until he received a sign from his lord that he had arrived in the right place. After many miles the halter broke and some nearby harvesters started to laugh at him, so he cursed their field, proclaiming that it would always rain when they cut the hay, and it promptly started to rain hard. Cuthmann repaired his halter and walked further until he came to a field at the base of a hill surrounded by two streams, where it broke again; this he took as the sign to stop. He built a wooden hut for his mother and then went on to build a church. No one knows a date for this story or the date the church was originally built, but Cuthmann was certainly known for his miraculous powers. *Cuth* in Old English means familiar, intimate, related or friendly and Man is a rune name we've looked at previously, so the name Cuthmann very possibly means a familiar, intimate, related person – which fits in well with Ing.

So what does Ing mean to you?

This rune has its roots way back in time and it must have been understood by the early English even though most of its meaning seems lost today. Read the verse again and note down what you think. There is much more to be learned about the wagon cult, so further research can be undertaken; you will find lots of information on the internet. However, remember not to take everything as the truth, as it is all just opinion, but some of these opinions may ring true to you and help you

The Futhorc

with your understanding. What do you think about the wagon rites? What about at the aspect of fertility – how do you feel about it? What do you think happened during the Nerthus rites mentioned by Tacitus? This rune has so much information just bubbling beneath the surface for you to discover.

Ēðel - Homeland

Eðel byþ oferleof æghwylcum men,
gif he mot ðær rihtes and gerysena on
bruca on bolde bleadum oftast.

Homeland is very dear to every man
if there rightfully and with propriety he may
enjoy wealth in his dwelling generally.

This rune has the phonemic value of /ɜː/, as in the 'ea' at the beginning of earth. It is sometimes written œðel, which shows a diphthong at the beginning; for this reason the rune is pronounced 'earth-el' with a long 'er' at the beginning and not like the feminine name Ethel.

This verse is about homeland in two senses, the first being your personal estate by inheritance or inherited wealth and the other concerning the land where you and/or your ancestors were born, and where you share the feeling of belonging: your native land. On close inspection both translations seem to allude to two slightly different versions of homeland. It is not that obvious on first reading; what is obvious, though, is how important it was to everyone.

> *Native land is overdear to every man,*
> *if he there his rights and befitting (honour)*
> *may enjoy in his blood oftest with increase.*
> **Kemble**

In approaching homeland as inherited estate we need to look again at the early English and the laws that formed their society. Although this verse seems sided in men's favour, this isn't the case in reality because women also inherited. Family land was passed through the generations within some very complex kinship groups and the early English were very flexible in their inheritance laws. Generally, land and possessions were

The Futhorc

passed to sons first but where there were no sons, daughters would inherit. The mortality rate at the time was very high and statistically it was likely that if you, as a couple, gave birth to six children you would only have one son who survived his father. Also, 20 per cent of couples would only have daughters.

Inheritance was divided or partitioned among sons first, but this partitioning was not necessarily equal. The laws governing how the partitions were made up were usually local and often influenced by individual circumstances. In the charters of King Ecgberht there is an example of partitioning between daughters where a father left ten hides of land and the king decided that the three surviving daughters could partition it between themselves as they wished. They decided that they would take an equal portion each, but later one of the daughters decided to move to Devon and her partition was divided between the remaining two.

Homeland as the land of your birth and your ancestors has a slightly different meaning today than it did to the early English. Today it is more a feeling of belonging to a place you feel at home in and a longing to return to that place when you are away; it isn't so much the actual physical tie of birth and family. People naturally live in smaller communities so to create a very large community is very difficult, and to establish one where everyone is happy to live under the same laws and love their neighbours as family does not always go smoothly. Many Governments around the world have tried, and are still trying – often with much success – to encourage this sense of homeland, but it is not so easy for large countries and sometimes these societies are in danger of breaking down. You can see this in large countries over recent years: for example, the collapse of the old USSR and Yugoslavia, where one moment we could all see a country and society that seemed to work well and the next moment there was a bloodbath as society broke down into different factions.

In early societies their tribal lands were smaller and tied by blood and family; as such, they were very important and needed to be defended against others. In Britain you can find ancient tribal boundaries and markers such as hill forts and the earlier cross-dykes. Archaeologists are still debating and developing ideas about their actual uses but territory markers seem a strong contender. Many of us have the idea of early man staying in one place when in fact many travelled on business or in exploration, although it seems they would always return to their native land if they could, especially if it was in danger. These tribal homelands were places where you could feel totally at home: everyone was working towards the same outcome, and you needed to survive together by growing food, by hunting, and by following the same spiritual beliefs and unwritten tribal laws. The Aboriginal tribes of Australia had and still have their Dreamtime and songs of the land, in which all of the information about their native land is stored. The singing of these songs strengthens the bonds of the people to their homeland.

So what does Eðel mean to you?

This rune is quite simple, but as with all the runes it can lead you into further study through the ideas it sparks. To find out the meaning it has for you, consider your relationship with the place in which you live. Do you feel part of your local community? How many neighbours do you know? Do you share any common interests? Note all of this in your journal and then have a think about a place that you long to return to. Do you have a holiday destination you visit regularly? Is there a place you have visited that you long to visit again or one you would like to move to, and why? The Welsh have a word *hiraeth* that doesn't translate directly into English; people often take it to mean homesickness, but it is more than this: it is a very deep longing for, and bond to, your homeland. Consider whether the Eðel rune verse could express this type of bond. You may find the idea of community interesting – perhaps either living in a community or aiming to. You can read up on others' experiences of living in a community, talk to those who do, and even volunteer within a community that is self-reliant. Many communities encourage volunteers during busy times.

What about inherited land? Do you know anyone who has been left property by their family? How do these people feel about their property? Visit a large house, such as a manor house with land, and imagine what it would be like to call it your home. How would you cope with all of the work? How would you show your pride in your homeland? Can you relate this to how early peoples must have felt? Most of us today are unlikely to inherit land but with some imagination and the right questions we might experience what it would be like.

Dæg - Day

Dæg byþ drihtnes sond, deore mannum,
mære metodes leoht, myrgþ and tohiht
eadgum and earmum, eallum brice.

Day is the Lord's sending, dear to men,
god's splendid light, joy and hope
to the blessed and the wretched, a benefit to all.

This rune has the phonemic value of /d/ - 'd' as it is in day - and in fact the rune can be pronounced 'day'. The 'æ' sounds like the 'a' in apple and the 'g' sound in Old English has three sounds: the 'g' in gold, the 'y' in yule and the soft 'g' or /ɣ/ used in the middle of a word such as Sigel and Lagu.

This rune verse is a very simple one: day is sent by the Lord, and is a great glorious light that gives mirth and hope to everyone - rich and poor. For the early English the day started at sunset the night before: for example, Tuesday night would have started at sunset on Monday. This verse concentrates on day as in daylight and although it is the Lord's sending it can just as well mean a pre-Christian lord of light as it can the Christian God.

Day is the Lord's messenger, dear to men,
the glorious light of God, mirth and consolation
to rich and poor, useful to all.
Kemble

Everything seems so much better in the light of day; there are monsters that hide in the night, and it was very rare for people in early English times to stray from their settlements after dark. The light of the sun also brings warmth which is of benefit to everyone. In the north summer days are longer which enables everyone to work longer hours. Working on the land, making things for the home and cooking are so much easier when you can see, but trying to make and mend during the winter by firelight or candlelight is almost impossible. For early society the main meal, dinner, was eaten at midday so that the cooking could be done in daylight. Today, even though we have artificial lighting and are able to work in the dark, we look forward to the summer when days are longer and we don't have to travel to and from work in the dark. We go out and get together with friends more often during lighter evenings, but we naturally tend towards staying indoors on dark winter nights.

Most esoteric rune books consider the words day and daylight for this rune but Jacob Grimm identified that a god called Bældæg had a connection to it. After Grimm associated him with day it in turn led him to identify Bældæg with a deity of light: the shining one or white one. Bældæg is the Old English form of Baldur, one of Odin's sons, who was the most beautiful and charming boy. Bældæg as Woden's son can be found in some English kings lists but there is nothing left to link him with a cult following in early English society. This deity though has links with Bel, Belenus, Beli Mawr, Balor and others, all solar deities whose early origins were likely to be Indo-European and who migrated across Europe from the south, around Turkey and Greece, and into Britain and Ireland, probably via the Belgae Tribes of the south-east of England during the 1st century BCE.

These connections lead us to look at the 'god of light', who is usually indestructible apart from a small and very unlikely vulnerability. This god is a warrior who is tricked by an opponent who has discovered his vulnerability; he then dies, but will come back at an appointed time. This is a very broad outline of the story, of which there are many versions across Europe, including Britain and Ireland: they vary in content, but seem to follow the same general theme. When the idea of Bældæg is applied to this verse it tells us that the daylight is sent by Bældæg, who gives his great glorious light and offers mirth and hope to everyone, rich and poor.

So what does Dæg mean to you?

This rune can be taken very simply as day, as in the period of time during the daylight hours, but what does the day shine a light on? Most of us are familiar with the idea that things 'come to light' and that something that confused you becomes 'clear in the light of day'. How does this rune connect to night time, if at all? Make notes in your journal when you are kept awake by confusing thoughts at night and note how different these thoughts are come the morning.

Can you think of any of the solar deity myths and legends? The information above is an introduction to this idea and can be followed up by your own research: there is lots of information on the internet. If you are interested you can read the story of Baldur from the Scandinavian sources and then see how this might be linked to the British stories in the *Mabinogi*, stories made popular by Lady Charlotte Guest in her book *The Mabinogion*. Also look at the Irish mythologies and find the connections. You may already be familiar with many of these stories but have you looked closely at their relatedness?

Āc - Oak

Ac byþ on eorþan elda bearnum
flæsces fodor, fereþ gelome
ofer ganotes bæþ; garsecg fandaþ
hwæþer ac hæbbe æþele treowe.

Oak is for the sons of men on earth
a feeder of flesh, often travels
over gannet's bath, the ocean tests
whether the oak keeps good faith.

This rune has the phonemic value of /ɔ:/, which sounds somewhere between the 'ah' and 'oa' in oar. The rune is pronounced with a long sound as above and with a 'k' sound at the end.

This is the first of the runes that are additional to the Elder Futhark: in essence they have been created to reflect the changes in the sounds of Old English from those used in the lands of the other Old Germanic tongues. We should not consider these runes less valuable than the earlier 24, as they still have names assigned and verses to describe them. As you can see the first of these runes is Oak.

When you read this verse, it seems rather strange: it is difficult to see how oak can be a feeder of flesh and then travel over the ocean where it is tested on its good faith. This indicates that it may be one of the riddle verses and that we need to take a step back and consider the verse without the word 'oak'. What could possibly be a feeder of flesh as well as something seafaring boats are made of? Both Pollington and Kemble's translations agree, so it seems there is no extra information hidden in the language itself.

The Futhorc

Oak is on earth to the sons of men
food of the flesh, often he goeth
over the gannet's bath, tempteth the ocean,
he that hath oak the noble tree.
Kemble

Regarding a 'feeder of flesh', there is a very old practice known as pannage, which is the right of people to put their pigs into the local forest or woodland to fatten them on the fallen acorns, beechmast, chestnuts and any other nuts. The word 'pannage' comes from French and Latin, so does not have its roots in Old English, but it is mentioned in the *Domesday Book* and therefore is very likely to reflect a practice that was common before the book was compiled. There is only one place in Britain that still practises pannage, and that is the New Forest in Hampshire. Pigs were a very important food to the early peoples of Britain and they were also considered sacred. A pig's head was usually the most important dish presented at the midwinter feast and recently it has been discovered by archaeologists that young pigs (at about nine months of age) were eaten as the main source of meat during the Neolithic celebrations at Stonehenge. Wild pigs and domesticated pigs are found in the old British tales, usually with a magical connection, and they were venerated by the early English, shown by the uses of the boar in their artwork, including on the Sutton Hoo helmet.

The gannet is a bird commonly found around coasts and harbours, a fine fisherman that flies underwater to catch its food, so 'over the gannets bath' is a nice poetic description of the type of environment in which the ocean tests how well oak has been used to build boats. Oak must be one of the most iconic trees used in the building of boats in England, known for its strength and resistance to rotting. Famously many of the ships in Nelson's fleet at the Battle of Trafalgar were built from trees sourced in the Forest of Dean, and after visiting there in 1803 he requested that the Admiralty plant more oaks. They did, and these so-called Trafalgar Oaks flourished, with some recently used to restore the timbers of his flagship the HMS *Victory*.

The oak is the national symbol of many countries and is connected with strength and endurance, and it had – and still has – an especially strong connection with the ancient Germanic peoples through Donar's Oak. Donar's Oak is Thor's Oak, which the Romans named Jove's Oak, and it shows the early peoples' veneration of trees and groves. The oak was dedicated to Thor and could also be connected to the Irminsul, a column or tree trunk raised in the open air. Some think the sacred tree at Uppsala, which is often seen as the mythic World Tree, was an oak. The oak was worshipped by the Indo-Europeans and connected to a thunder or lightening god, so it is no surprise to find it associated both with Thor of the Germanic peoples and Taranis of the Gallic peoples. The etymology of the word 'druid' is connected to the Proto-Celtic word for oak, and druids and oak trees go hand in hand.

It is interesting to observe that the oak, the ash and the yew are all connected with the idea of the World Tree, and in *The Old English Rune Poem* Æsc follows Ac, which in turn is followed by a bow made of yew.

So what does Ac mean to you?

The oak is a sacred tree to so many, but how does it make you feel? What do you instantly associate with oak? Write this down in your journal, because your first thoughts are often the strongest associations. To find out more about the oak you can investigate its history further in books, at the library and on the internet, but don't forget to go and have a chat with one. Do you have an oak near to where you live? Perhaps you have a favourite oak tree that you sit with and share your thoughts with. Once again, Penny Billington's book can help you to gain a deeper relationship with this beautiful tree.

This rune is connected to the pig via its acorns, and this allows for further research into the magical connections with pigs as well as the practical ones. You may also want to look at how the gods Thor and Taranis have connections with the oak. All of this will help you build a strong connection to the meaning of this rune.

Æsc - Ash

ᚫ

Æsc biþ oferheah, eldum dyre
stiþ on staþule, stede rihte hylt,
ðeah him feohtan on firas monige.

Ash is very tall, dear to men,
strong in foundations, holds its place properly
though many men fight against it.

This rune has the phonemic value of /æ/, which sounds like the 'a' in apple or even ash and is how this rune is pronounced.

The verse tells us that Ash is very tall, or 'over high' and it is dear to men because it has many uses. The tree has strong roots which spread out from the tree, so it doesn't fall easily. Then the verse goes on to talk about many men fighting against it. Both translations agree, but it leaves a strange picture of people trying to fight ash trees.

Ash is over high dear to men,
stiff in its station well it holdeth its place,
although against it fight many men.
Kemble

Ash is a very useful tree: it grows straight and strong, and it is flexible. Its pliability is good enough for it to be used to make bows, and ash is often used when yew is unavailable. Ash is one of the toughest hardwoods and the trees were used by the early English to make bows and spears, as well as stockades, so at a very practical level it can be seen that ash was used in battle and defence. When an ash is surrounded by tall trees it grows very straight and high, while keeping a small trunk diameter. Ash can be shaped into a very sharp point, so when it was used for stockades the posts were placed both upright and angled outward to form a very strong defensive wall that held its place and injured those who rushed against it.

Many poems extol the virtues of ash as firewood and this is a verse from a traditional woodman's poem:

But ash logs, all smooth and grey,
Burn them green or old,
Buy up all that come your way,
They're worth their weight in gold.
Anon.

Ash grows moderately fast and is a useful wood for a variety of purposes. It does not splinter easily so it is useful for making handles for hammers, axes and spades; it is often used for furniture and coppices as well. Along with its burning properties this makes ash a very practical wood, as all of the offcuts and leftover pieces from woodworking can be burned on the fire.

This rune shape was originally found in verse 4 of the Elder Futhark, as Ansuz, but is now taken by Os in *The Old English Rune Poem* and this, as mentioned earlier, is due to the change in the sound of 'A'. There is a possibility that Æsc still contains some of the influence of Ansuz within it. Stephen Pollington, in his book *The Elder Gods: The Other World of Early England,* tells us that Æsc may have been known to the early English as a supernatural being. There was an early king of Kent called Oisc (which is a spelling variation of ash), who was said to be a descendant of Hengist, mentioned earlier when discussing Eh. There is a being in Norse mythology called Askr (meaning ash). Askr and Embla (possibly elm or vine) form part of a creation myth as a proto-human couple created from wood who survived a great flood by hiding in the World Tree. It has been observed that early European and Indo-European society had stories of 'first couples' who were created from trees or rock and as previously mentioned, the ash tree is itself is often viewed as the World Tree. A theory has also been mooted that behind the story of Askr and Embla could lie the creation of fire, with a masculine ash as the fire drill and a feminine vine as the wood block.

So what does Æsc mean to you?

One of the best ways to discover this rune meaning is to visit an ash tree and ask it questions. Write a list of questions you would like to ask and seek out an ash tree near you. You can take it an offering of water, from a well or from rainfall would be best, introduce yourself, and ask the ash if you can sit for a while and it keep company. When you feel relaxed and comfortable, perhaps with your back resting on the trunk, then you can ask your questions – and remember to be patient, as tree time appears much slower to us. Think about the tree you are with, think about your question and see if you receive any ideas or thoughts on the answer; you may even meditate and go on a journey with the tree spirit. Trees have a good memory for our histories, and they are connected to each other and to their past more readily than we are.

Consider the uses of ash today and in the past. Have you ever been to a woodland crafts show? Perhaps you could arrange a visit to a show; this will allow you the chance to speak to woodworkers and find out about the different woods you see. Ask them what they like about ash as a material. Research the old poems by woodmen about the best firewood, and if you get a chance perhaps you can burn some ash.

What do you feel about the connection of ash to the World Tree and other sacred mythologies? Explore the ideas of the World Tree and see what similarities and differences they hold. Following all of these suggestions will help you to build a really good knowledge of ash in both practical and esoteric ways. If nothing else, walk tall and be like an ash.

Yr - Bow of yew

Yr byþ æþelinga and eorla gehwæs
wyn and wyrþmynd, byþ on wicge fæger,
fæstlic on færelde, fyrdgeatewa sum.

Yew bow for every noble and warrior is
a joy and adornment, is fair on a steed
a trusty piece of wargear on a journey.

This rune has the phonemic value of /ü/, which has an 'ee' sound made with rounded lips; try saying 'oo' and then, without changing the shape of your mouth, say 'ee'. The rune is pronounced like this with a long sound and with a trilled 'R' at the end.

Both translations say the same thing: that the bow is part of warlike arms and fair on a horse. In the 14th and 15th centuries British longbow men were famed for their strength and skills; the English and Welsh could fire ten to twelve arrows in the time it took continental bowmen to fire five or six, and the best wood for a longbow is yew. During this time the majority of bowmen were on foot, which makes it difficult to imagine the use of a yew bow from horseback. However, it is easy to see that a good yew bow was a joy and a trusty piece of war gear for the early English or anyone prior to the invention of the gun, especially if you were travelling into unknown or unsafe territory.

> *Bow is of nobles and of every man*
> *joy and dignity, it is fair on the horse,*
> *firm in the expedition, part of warlike arms.*
> **Kemble**

The history of archery goes back a very long way - as far as the late Stone Age, or even the middle Stone Age - and seems to have occurred in most societies. The domestication of horses also has a long history, and with the two happening together it is logical that at some point people would

The Futhorc

have developed the skill of being able to simultaneously ride a horse and shoot a bow. The Celtic and Germanic peoples were famed for their affiliation with horses and the Mongols, Scythians and Huns were well-known for their horse archers – in fact, the Romans adopted horse archers into their cavalry ranks when they saw how effective they could be. When the Romans arrived in Britain much was reported about the British use of chariots, but there were no reports of horse archers in their histories, and it is likely that archers rode in these chariots. It is also known that the Romans stationed Sarmatian cavalrymen in Britain, some of whom stayed in the Lancashire area after the Romans left; it is very probable that they had horse archers in their ranks and that this skill was carried forward in Britain.

A horse archer using a bow is extremely skilled at riding and controlling the horse with just their legs as well as being strong and dexterous enough to fire a bow from an unsteady platform. They were a very fast and devastating force who were able to scout; enter skirmishes by attacking in short, sharp bursts; and protect foot soldiers. In the later Middle Ages the Germans and Scandinavians were famous for their mounted crossbow archers, who did just this; furthermore, in the height of battle, they would follow a skirmish by sword fighting from horseback.

So what does Yr mean to you?

It is a good idea to research further into the use of bows, especially English longbows. There is lots of information to be found on the internet, including video of mounted archers – take a look at the skills required. Have you ever used a bow? If not, perhaps you can find a taster session at a local club, or visit a historical re-enactment fayre or event where you can have a go at shooting one. It is fun, even if you miss the target: learning is all about experiencing, so don't think you need to be perfect.

Think about the aspect of yew in this rune; it already has its own rune, Eoh, so how does this use differ? Do you think this rune is really connected to yew? Bow stands quite happily as the name although Yr is the name for the yew rune in the Norse Rune Row. Remember that the Norwegian Rune Poem is thought to be much younger than *The Old English Rune Poem*. On a practical level this rune shape is created from Ur and Is and therefore it is a bind rune, i.e. more than one rune merged together. Go back over your notes and see what ideas this might offer you. How do you think it might influence your feeling for this rune?

Meditate on this verse; use your imagination to journey on horseback with a bow; use all of your senses to discover what you can. Don't forget to write down your thoughts and experiences in your journal.

Īar - Beaver

*Īar byþ eafix and ðeah a bruceþ
fodres on foldan, hafaþ fægerne eard
wætre beworpen, ðær he wynnum leofaþ.*

Beaver is a riverfish yet it always enjoys
food on land, has a fine dwelling
surrounded by water where it lives happily.

This rune has the phonemic value of /iɔ/, a diphthong that resembles 'ior' or 'your', although both are short sounds. It is usually pronounced with a long 'ī', which reminds me of 'Eeyore' from Winnie the Pooh.

The translation of this verse has developed since Kemble's time, and both translations are much the same, but the identity of the river fish caused difficulties, hence Kemble guessing at eel. Today there is still no certainty that it is a beaver, even though the description leads to this conclusion.

> *Eel (?) is a river fish, yet ever enjoyeth
> its food on the ground, a fair dwelling hath it
> surrounded with water, where it liveth in joy.*
> **Kemble**

The word Īar only appears in Old English as the name of this rune; it can't be translated directly into beaver and there is an old word for this animal. The old English word *Beofor* is related to the Welsh word *Befer*, and comes from the Indo-European word *Bhebhros*. This rune is not an Elder Futhark rune, it is a later rune added to the Futhorc to express changes in the English language. It does not seem to have developed from any of the Elder Futhark runes, although a bind rune of Is and Gyfu would look the same. It is highly likely that this verse, although obviously an observation of nature, is influenced by early Christian thought and practice.

We know that a beaver is a mammal and not a fish, and in Britain today we hardly consider the beaver as a native animal because they became extinct so long ago. We also know that eels do not eat on the ground but underwater. For over a thousand years English Christian society has been following the practice of fasting. Fasts and abstinence developed out of Old Testament practice and the early Church fasted on Wednesdays and Fridays. A fast allowed for one meal a day in the evening, and this meal could not contain flesh but could contain fish. Fish, of course, come from rivers and the sea and it is very likely that otters and beavers were considered fish because they also come from rivers and are edible. The old Christian tradition of fasting later developed into fasting on Fridays during Lent and then even later into the tradition of eating fish on Fridays. In the 17th century, the Catholic Church declared that beaver were fish, a decision that was probably based on Thomas Aquinas' 13th-century *Summa Theologica*, which included a basis of animal classification that relied on the habitat of an animal, not just its anatomy.

The otter builds its holt in the bank of a river, but a beaver's lodge is surrounded by water, usually a lake or pool created in a river by the beaver's dam. The lodge is built with entrances under water and a dry platform inside where the beaver can feed and bring up its young, just as the verse describes. Eurasian beavers were native in England up until the 12th century and possibly later in Scotland but were seldom seen there. In recent studies on beavers and their effect on the environment researchers have reported that fish grow bigger in the pools created by beaver dams and that the ecology around these pools is richer with more wildlife such as frogs, other small riverbank animals, and bugs. Along with this there tends to be clearer banking created by tree felling, which encourages a wider variety of plant life. Eurasian beavers have been reintroduced into Britain in some secure reserves in Scotland and Wales, and in 2014 beavers seemed to be reintroducing themselves in Devon.

During the time of the early English, beaver were found all over Britain and these animals probably held an important place in the sacred landscape. A beaver-tooth amulet has been found in an adolescent's grave in Watchfield, Oxfordshire. No one knows exactly why it was worn, but it was adorned with a gold setting so it was obviously highly valued. It could have been a charm to help with tooth problems or it could have

The Futhorc

been a totem animal much like boars, bears and wolves. As a totem animal the eating of its flesh would have only been sanctioned as part of a sacred ritual or act.

So what does Iar mean to you?

Looking just at the verse, do you think that it is about a beaver? If you do, what do you relate beaver to? Connect with the animal in any way you can, through study and/or meditation, and so on. If you can see beavers in their own natural habitat or perhaps in a good zoological park, this can be a good way of connecting, but remember to behave with great care and respect. If you are unable to visit in person, watch any videos or documentaries you can find.

Look at how beavers are used in language: the phrase 'beavering away' means working diligently at something. Do you feel this rune could be related to hard work? There is also slang usage for the word which may not seem right, but exists just the same; could you consider this in your interpretation?

What do you think of this rune shape as a bind rune of Is and Gyfu? Look at your journal notes about these two runes and see if you can find your interpretation of this as a bind rune? Ice and Gift make an interesting combination of their own, but can you also relate this to beaver? It doesn't need to be related but it is good practice and helps expand your thought processes.

Make a note of everything in your journal; you never know when your ideas and interpretations might apply even if rather unexpectedly.

Ēar - Grave, one of the sea or the earth

Ēar byþ egle eorla gehwylcun,
ðonn[e] fæstlice flæsc onginneþ,
hraw colian, hrusan ceosan
blac to gebeddan; bleda gedreosaþ,
wynna gewitaþ, wera geswicaþ.

Grave is frightful to every warrior
when the flesh begins inexorably
the corpse to cool, to embrace the earth
the dark as its companion; fruits fall away,
joys pass away, promises fail.

This rune has the phonemic value of /eɔ/, a diphthong that sounds like something between 'eh-ah' and 'eh-oa', but short and joined together into one sound. Diphthongs are not easy to imagine as sounds, but in modern English we use them all the time when we name the vowels such as 'A', 'O' and 'U'. Listen as you name these and you will find two vowel sounds in each letter name.

The rune name is translated slightly differently, with Pollington identifying the rune name as Grave and Kemble as War, but the rest of the verse is only stylistically different. Although Kemble was born into a famous acting family he would have been acutely aware of the horrors of war as it was prolific during his lifetime; he was born during the Napoleonic Wars and there were plenty of other face-to-face combat wars to follow. As far as I know, he did not serve as a soldier, but he was politically involved in an attempt to bring about a democratic revolution in Spain. Pollington, as a writer of today, has the advantage of 150 years' further academic study and names the rune as a Grave, of earth or sea. Either way, this rune indicates the end of a life.

The Futhorc

*War is a terror to every man,
when continually the flesh beginneth
the corpse to cool, to choose the earth
pale for its consort, its joys depart
its pleasures vanish, it parteth from men.*
Kemble

The *Bosworth-Toller Anglo-Saxon Dictionary* has an ocean, a wave, a harrow, an ear and an ear of corn as meanings of Ēar. These meanings show the connection of this rune with both the earth and the sea. The verse is very earthbound and can be taken literally as a grave within the earth, but it could also be a riddle for a sea burial or a ship burial. With the meaning of harrow as a farm implement, we can see a clear connection to the earth and its preparation for crops; this is found in the *Bosworth-Toller Anglo-Saxon Dictionary*, but originally came from Arthur S. Napier's *Anecdota Oxoniensa, Old English Glosses*.

This verse clearly indicates that death and the return of life to the earth is the meaning of this rune. It is a very difficult topic to deal with and is often a taboo subject, but it is an inevitable part of life and something we must all face for our loved ones, our friends and ourselves. To the early English warriors described in this verse it was better to die in battle than to die of old age and feel helpless and useless at the end. There was a glory to death in battle, as you would be remembered for your bravery and get your just rewards in the afterlife – but would people remember your past accolades when you died of old age? Even the rune shape can be connected to Tīr, with the ends of the arrow arms folding back up. Tiw the god of war and judgement: how would he judge the warrior who did not die in battle?

This rune shape can also serve as a reminder of the Irminsul (*Eormensyl* in Old English), the mighty column of the Continental Saxons that seems to represent the World Tree. This was very sacred and it is thought that sacrifices were made at the Irminsul. Interestingly, this can allow for a very loose, possibly romantic, connection with the word 'harrow', but in another sense. The name Harrow on the Hill, the place where the famous Harrow Boys' School is found, comes from a word indicating a heathen temple. Its name in the Domesday Book was 'Herges', which developed from the name Guminga-hergae, meaning heathen temple. The names look very different now, but when you pronounce the name *hergae* in Old English is sounds very similar to harrow. Harrow has several meanings, one of which is to harry, and this comes from the Old English word *hergian*, which also means pillage, plunder, ravage, waste, devastate, make an incursion or a raid – and also to make war.

So what does Ēar mean to you?

The primary meaning of this verse is death, which is one of the most frightening things we have to face. What does death mean to you? Have you ever discussed it with friends and family? Do you have a funeral plan in place? What if you have an accident? Will all of your wishes be catered for? What will your family do? With so many questions on a subject we don't want to discuss, it can make it easy to put to one side for now. It is worthwhile noting your reactions to death as well as the reactions of others in your journal. One major thing that death does is change things, and people will often use a reference to death as a reference to great change. Have you ever had your tarot cards read? Did the death card appear in your reading? If so, note in your journal how you felt if it did appear, or how you may have felt if it had appeared.

Look at the other meanings of the word 'ear' that you can relate to this rune. You may find an ear of corn reminds you of Lammas or Lughnasagh celebrations of the harvest, perhaps even the spirit of the corn, often called John Barleycorn. Have a listen to the words of the song 'The Ballad of John Barleycorn' from Damh the Bard's album *The Hills They Are Hollow*, and see what you find there.

Our ears should be used for listening. Do you think this rune may indicate a need to listen? There are a lot of meanings linked to this rune and you should note how these resonate with you. Remember, though, that even if they don't resonate now they may at some point in the future, so note everything you can in your journal.

Part 3

Wyrd

What is Wyrd?

Wyrd is very difficult to describe. It is something you need to experience with your senses and, through them, your soul. Wyrd is an Anglo-Saxon word and today it is generally considered to mean fate or destiny. Wyrd is found in Old English literature, examples of which are:

Gǣð ā Wyrd swā hīo scel! – Wyrd always goes as she shall! (Beowulf)

Wyrd bið ful arǣd! – Wyrd is completely relentless! ('The Wanderer', The Exeter Book, 10th century)

Me þæt wyrd gewæf – Wyrd wove this for me. ('The Rhyming Poem', The Exeter Book, 10th century)

The idea of Wyrd, or something close to this, can found worldwide in various forms, but you will see it most clearly as the Fates, the Norns and the Wyrd Sisters – a name made famous by Terry Pratchett. The Norns are called Verðandi, Skuld and Urðr, which in Old English are: *Weorðende* – becoming, or turning; *Scyld* – what is owed, an obligation, a necessity, a debt; and *Wyrd* – what has become, what has happened, what is completed. It is likely that the idea of the Wyrd Sisters is a later association because the early English usually only mention Wyrd as a complete, feminine entity in their writings. The meanings are all there in Old English and Stephen Pollington tells us in his book *The Elder Gods: The Otherworld of Early England*:

Time flows from Weorðende to Wyrd with Scyld influencing its passage.'

You will find Wyrd is much more complex than fate. It is more flexible and is not set until it is finally played out: there's everything to play for until 'the fat lady sings' as they say.

So Wyrd can be seen as the flow of time and it can also be expressed as the Well of Wyrd. This well is not so much a deep hole in the ground with water at the bottom, but a well spring. In this spring you see the water as a still pool on the surface, but when you look more deeply you will see that it moves in constant eddies with mesmerising patterns as water rises from beneath. People just passing can only see a still pond, but there is more going on beneath the surface and changes to this flow can transform the environment of the whole area.

Spinners and weavers are also terms used widely to describe the Wyrd Sisters, Norns or Fates. These 'weavers of fate' can be envisioned as spinning threads from the moment of your birth, where you are tied into life; and at your death, when the threads are cut, the pattern that you created still exists. Between these two great events, your life thread is woven together with the threads of other people, events and places to set your story like a woven cloth. Your cloth is part of a living loom known as the 'Wyrd'. All the warp threads – the long threads that go from top to bottom in a traditional loom – are tied to absolutely everything that exists around us, both seen and unseen. Some of these, but not all for most mortals, are used in the pattern of your own life.

How does this weaving work? Most of us learned about looms with a fixed number of warp and weft threads that you can use to make a scarf or long, even piece of material. Does this picture sound like Wyrd with all its possibilities? There is very old type of weaving, a type found all around the world, which is still being used today. It only uses warp threads that are knotted together to create the cloth. It is known in northern Europe as 'sprang', and interestingly creates a stretchy cloth like a net. If you experiment with sprang you may see it as much closer to Wyrd. Sprang is usually made with one warp thread and you can create an even cloth, but you can also make holes and patterns by missing threads or clumping some together. By bringing threads from other points in the cloth – or even from another cloth – it may even be possible to create more multi-dimensional pieces.

Scientists have mathematical formulae and models that describe the effects of Wyrd, which often seem to happen for no reason and appear chaotic. They call it 'the butterfly effect', where a butterfly beating its wings can become the cause of a hurricane on the other side of the world. Chaos is one of the effects of Wyrd: the things you do affect your connections to everything, seen and unseen. Through magic and developing our connection to Wyrd we can become more conscious of the effect of our lives. You can learn to feel the threads, touch them and influence them.

Let's recap

Wyrd is what is happening right now; it is not set until the moment is complete. For example, you are reading this and so our threads in Wyrd have been linked. It could have been different though: a necessity or obligation could have influenced you to have a cup of coffee, go to the shops or do some gardening, and you may not have bought this book to read. But this part of the journey is now set in Wyrd and we are both

Wyrd

moving forward with new choices to be made, which will be influenced by other necessities and obligations. Some of these are the same but some could be created by our new thread connections in your cloth.

Wyrd is connected to everything and everyone. It is living and constantly changing. It is part of a concept where everything has its own life and purpose and should be valued as such. The web of every life can be seen as long threads that are part of the body and which are attached to, and part of, the Web of Wyrd. These threads will be joined to other threads as you live your life: the threads of the people you meet, decisions you make and events that happen. In some cases you will feel unable to change things that are happening – fate goes as she must – but at other times you will feel free to choose. Wyrd sets the pattern of your life as you are living it: your future hasn't happened yet.

Runes and Wyrd

It seems that runes, as Cornelius Tacitus told us in his account of Germania, have always been used to connect with Wyrd. They offer clues about what may happen going forward and so inform your choices when they do.

Reading *The Old English Rune Poem* gives you a head start, and you will already be seeing the connections. The early English loved their games of chance, as indicated by the rune Peorð and evidenced by the gaming pieces found in graves. Did these gaming pieces help them decide which steps to take by showing them the course of Wyrd? Using runes can help you look at the course of Wyrd and, perhaps, like the early English, influence it by nudging it in a more favourable direction.

Each rune is connected to a different aspect of Wyrd, and by learning from the experience of the early English you are, by extension, learning your connections to everything. Runes are a key that you can use to unlock and influence Wyrd and you can do this with runecraft by employing the methods of Galdor (an incantation, divination, enchantment, a charm, magic, sorcery, *Bosworth-Toller Anglo-Saxon Dictionary*) which you can explore later on in this book. But first it's time to experience Wyrd with our souls.

Touching Wyrd - exercises to explore your connection with Wyrd

To work with Wyrd, the very moment that your life pattern is woven, is very much a 'live in the moment' experience: feel the now, slow it down and explore it. Once you have achieved this, you can look at how you can influence your future. This is exactly what this exercise will help you to achieve. In order to touch Wyrd and to make any sense of it you must use all of your senses. We will start by using our senses of hearing, smell, taste and touch. These will help you slow down your life for a moment and experience the now in full colour. You must give yourself time and be patient with yourself.

I have used the word exercises, plural, as you can do this either in one go or in bite-size pieces. Sometimes the thought of trying to slow down into a meditative state can seem impossible, but practice makes perfect: the more you practise the clearer it all becomes. It may take several attempts, because we rush so much these days it's difficult to slow down and listen with our bodies. This is all part of what we now call mindfulness and you can find lots of help in achieving it, but if you find sitting still and meditating difficult you can try it while walking, although you need to have your eyes open. When using the walking meditation method you should relax your visual focus so that you are aware of dangers, and so on, but you are not actually looking at anything in particular.

To start find somewhere outside to sit by yourself; you don't need to be totally alone and the most important thing is to feel comfortable. How about sitting in your garden or the local park? Don't choose a day that is rough and uncomfortable, too hot or too cold, too wet or too windy. Find a seat that is perhaps a little sheltered so that you are protected from extremes but which still enables you to experience the natural world.

- Begin by closing your eyes and taking some deep, slow breaths; relax with your 'out' breath, and imagine all of your conscious day-to-day life drifting away from you.

- When you feel ready, take an inward look at your breath, the air that you are breathing: can you smell anything? It could be the trees, it could be flowers, it could even be smoke from a fire or exhaust fumes - anything at all.

- Can you taste the aroma you can smell? How does that feel? What does it remind you of? Do you taste anything else?

- Next, notice a distant noise; what does this remind you of, and where is it? It could be children playing, someone mowing the lawn, a fast car – what is it?

- Now concentrate on what you can feel: the sun on your skin, a breeze, or perhaps light drizzle. How does it make you feel?

I have not asked you to open your eyes and use the sense of sight, but this can come later; for now it is better to see with your inner or third eye. By using your other senses you can begin to make connections along the threads of Wyrd that you will travel along in your imagination.

When you are comfortable with the exercise above, see if you can find the source of a noise or smell. Choose something that is quite close to you and imagine you can see a fine sparkling thread between you and the source of your interest. Travel along the thread with your mind and find the source. What is it? Does it have a colour? If you feel it is right, can you reach out and touch it? What does it feel like? Move back along the thread to yourself and relax again.

Don't forget to write your experiences down in your journal. Eventually you will be able to see and feel the threads to everything without having to think about it and with further practice you will be able to see them with your eyes open.

Can we influence Wyrd?

After reading this chapter so far you may be of the belief that it isn't possible to change Wyrd. The Old English phrases, especially the following two, definitely give this impression.

Gǣð ā Wyrd swā hīo scel! – Wyrd always goes as she shall!
Beowulf

Wyrd bið ful aræd! - Wyrd is completely relentless!
'The Wanderer', *The Exeter Book*, 10th Century

Many who experience it will find this impression true, and it would be misguided, for example, to advise that all who suffer from long-term medical conditions or have suffered injury beyond their control can be totally cured. Influencing Wyrd is not about a total change, it is about subtle change: a change that can make the outcome a little more favourable.

The word Wyrd is used today to describe the whole process of connection and life, but originally it described the actual moment that a life event becomes fixed in the woven fabric of time. When influencing Wyrd we are really considering the moment in time just before it is fixed.

> *Time flows from Weorðende to Wyrd with Scyld influencing its passage.'*
> **Stephen Pollington, The Elder Gods**

This means that what is happening or is going to happen in life will be influenced by Scyld before it becomes fixed in the weave.

Looking at Scyld

Scyld is pronounced 'shild', with an 'oo' lip shape, and it is the basis for our modern English word 'should'. In order to consider influencing Wyrd we need to consider Scyld and how this affects us all.

According to the *Bosworth-Toller Anglo-Saxon Dictionary*, Scyld means

1. guilt, sin, crime, or fault, and

2. a debt or due.

These words do not immediately fit with our concept of should today, but let's take a moment to look at each of these in turn and consider them at the point we need to make a decision.

> **Fault** – You have been asked to help someone and it clashes with other plans; you would normally say no, but you know that this person only needs help because of something you did. Should you help them because you think it is your fault?

> **Crime** – You are out shopping and you see something small that you really want, but can't quite afford. Should you commit the crime of shoplifting? It's only something small, you've checked it isn't tagged – you could take it and get away with it.

> **Sin** – You have broken one of your moral codes and it was against your best friend. You now find it incredibly difficult to face them, but you must. Can you go forward and keep your friendship, or has it been destroyed by your choice to sin?

Guilt - You have loving but demanding parents who have always harboured a dream for you to become a doctor; you are capable of doing so, but really you want to be a travel journalist. Will you let your future be coloured by your parents or can you overcome the guilt you feel and go your own way?

A debt - Someone has done you a favour or loaned you some money. You have a chance to repay the debt, but another, perhaps more interesting, opportunity arises. Should you repay what is owed or should you take up the opportunity and just vow to pay your debt later? You might even decide to ignore the debt completely.

Due - You plan your life around something you feel is your right or due, perhaps an inheritance or job promise, and you are sure it's an outcome you can rely on. Then it is given to someone else and all your plans fail. How will you move forward with this outcome and the betrayal you feel?

Our whole lives are coloured by things we think we should do; some of them are more important and a stronger influence than others, but ultimately the decision on what we will do is our choice alone. I am not advocating always taking the selfish option - it may not be morally correct and might not be the way to behave in society - but there could be occasion to do so. We should not ignore our promises or the people that help us. We must remember though that no choice is invalid and sometimes we need to make choices that will not necessarily be to our benefit.

Anyone can influence the course of Wyrd - in fact, we do it all the time by deciding what to do next. What we need to be aware of is that we may also make the decision not to decide for ourselves and let things roll because it appears easier. Peer pressure is probably one of the strongest decision-makers there is: we don't want to look bad in front of the people we want to like us. It's easier to go with the crowd than to be picked on for being different. When we are young we don't realise we have a choice because our adults make that choice, but gradually we learn and if we are lucky we have adults who help us see the choices and the consequences. Ultimately everything we meet on our life journey requires us to make our own decisions.

Using runes to influence Wyrd

Runes are a living force; they hold a shape that is recognised by Wyrd along with their sound. The choice of the words that go with the letter sounds of the runes is no haphazard accident: these words each have a meaning and energy that is also recognised within the Web of Wyrd. Runes have a life of their own and we have been getting to know that life; we are building a relationship with them and learning from them.

In the next chapter you will learn how to make runes. These runes are a physical representation of the shape and meaning of each rune within Wyrd. Even if you are unable to make your own runes, it is a good idea to read this chapter as it contains valuable information about forming a relationship with your set of runes.

Think about it!

Influencing Wyrd with magical intervention is not something to undertake lightly and probably one of the most important lessons you learn in the world of magic is not to take magical intervention as a first choice. Just because you can, doesn't mean you should.

Before you decide to influence Wyrd, the best course of action would be to find out more about the situation – and this is where divination is important. This is a great method of asking questions and getting to the root of the matter; even if you don't believe in divination, you will find that working with runes makes you ask questions you hadn't thought about. You can find out more about this in the next chapter. Once you have decided there is a good case for influencing Wyrd, then you can choose different ways to use talismans and amulets, which may contain plain runes, bind runes or mirror runes. Another method is Galdor, which is voicing the runes and sending them along the threads of the web to their destination.

Sometimes the decision to influence Wyrd is instinctive and simple – an example of this is as a good luck charm. You could make a talisman or amulet, use Galdor to charge it, and then give it to the person concerned. Remember, though, that you should always remind them that the gods will only aid those who make their own effort, and the charm will be for nothing if they don't.

Part 4

Making and working with runes

How to make your own runes

Wherever possible you should make your own runes and, according to runologists, these should be made from the wood of a fruit-bearing tree. It is suggested that a fruit-bearing tree means a tree that produces any fruit or nuts. The earliest evidence we have that seems to be related to runes is from Cornelius Tacitus in his work *Germania*. He was a great historian and is believed to be the son of the Cornelius Tacitus who was procurator of Germania and Belgi[c]a.

> *Their method is a simple one: they cut a branch from a fruit-bearing tree and divide it into small pieces which they mark with certain distinctive signs.*
> Cornelius Tacitus, Germania

Choosing the wood

The best wood to use is from a tree that you have a connection with. My set of runes is made from a rowan tree in my parents garden. I can remember it always being there, but I didn't realise how important it was to me until my father cut it down. I explained to him how upset I was and every time I visited I would ask him why and how he could have cut down such a beautiful tree. I realised then that I needed to keep a connection to the tree and asked for some branches. I am very pleased to say that the rowan tree is re-growing from the roots that were left behind and I often go and chat when I visit. If you do not have a tree that you are close to then maybe it is time to go and make connections in your locality or in a favourite place.

Working with trees is very powerful magic. We have spoken about meditating with trees when looking at the runes of yew, birch, oak and ash. Trees are living beings and it is worth treating them as you would treat another human, even though they live at a much slower pace than we do. They speak to each other by releasing chemical pheromones and also through the mycelium around their roots, and there are many trees such as the aspen and the yew that grow in families, literally connected by their roots and branches. Creating a relationship with the tree that your runes are cut from will help you form a very strong magical alliance with the spirit of that tree.

Cutting your runes

There are many ideas and traditions about how and when you should cut the wood from a tree that you want to use in a magical partnership. Some say to only cut a tree during the winter when the sap has withdrawn, others say it should be in spring before the fruit starts to form. Whatever tradition you decide to follow, or if you are using your instinct to decide, it is worth remembering that you need to connect with the essence of the tree - the dryad or tree spirit - because their aid is vital.

Remember that the tree will be giving you a gift and you may wish to leave a gift in exchange. There are many tales of how people accidentally cut themselves and then take this as payment due, but it may be more appropriate to plant another tree of the same species or to keep a promise to protect trees that are in danger. Other gifts are perfectly acceptable and a good example is the gift of your voice in song. Remember Gyfu and the responsibilities involved in gift giving.

The runes can be cut as disks from a branch about 1 inch or 2.25 cm in diameter, or as oblong tiles cut from larger pieces. They can also be made as staves from smaller twigs - about a little finger's width in diameter - by cutting a flat section into them to be marked with the runes; this method enables you to use several different trees. The cutting of the individual pieces is the first step in creating an entity or entities that will be your rune set, and you will need to create 29 of them. It is worth considering creating a few more in case some do not work out when you mark them, and of course if you don't need them for this rune set then you may want to create something you can wear, or save them for other magical practice.

The reason for referring to the runes as an entity or entities is based on an animistic belief that everything has its own life force, and that the relationship between you and the tree spirit is creating another life, the rune set, or lives, the individual runes. Everything is connected to everything in Wyrd.

Marking your runes

This is the most difficult part and requires patience and concentration, as there are 29 Old English runes and they are all slightly different but also very similar. It is easy to make a mistake but this is all part of creating the entity or entities that are your rune set.

Making and working with runes

The rune shapes can be carved into the rune using handheld woodworking tools or even using a handheld rotary tool such as a Dremel. You may wish to draw the runes on first with a pencil to help guide your hand. There are some who prefer to use pyrography to mark their runes and this can be done fairly cheaply by using a soldering iron to burn the rune shapes or you may wish to use a speciality pyrography pen. You may find yourself using paint or marker pen to mark your runes, and this is just as valid: you should mark them in a way that feels right for you.

What if I can't make my own runes?

If you are unable to make your own runes - and this could be for any reason, from health or limited space to lack of tools or even confidence - don't worry, as you may have a friend who can help or you might be able to track down a rune maker. The Old English runes are particularly difficult to source; there are many that sell Anglo-Saxon runes but I have often found that they are in fact an Elder Futhark set with English rune shapes. There are some rune makers who will make a set to your specifications, or you can find some on my webpage www.suzannerance.co.uk. The ones I supply are made of fruit-bearing woods, have the runes carved on them and are specifically left in a basic state so that you can mark with pyrography or paint and charge them yourself.

Charging your runes

There are some runologists who like to start charging their runes as they are marking them, and some do this by performing Galdor over each rune as they work on them. There is a section on Galdor later in this book.

Once you have made your runes you will need to charge them magically and many runologists believe that the most important thing here is to blood them. This is adding an essence of yourself into your runes to blend with the essence of the tree and this action gives them life. It does not require a lot of blood and the safest way of doing this is to get hold of a medical finger-pricking lancet (these are available on the internet), or you may know someone that is diabetic who is able to let you have an unused one from their blood-testing kit. You may find that in the process of making your runes you cut or prick yourself accidentally - it is amazing how often this happens. You can put a small drop on each rune or you may prefer to add it to the oils you use to dress your runes.

Dressing your runes can be as simple as finding some olive oil to wipe your runes with or you may wish to create an oil by adding some herbs. My favourite herb oil for this is mugwort, whose properties are excellent for lucid dreaming and so ideal for the connection with Wyrd and for divination. Mugwort is found in the Old English herbal, *The Lacnunga*, in the first line of 'Woden's Nine Herbs Charm':

> Remember mugwort, what you revealed/ what you set out in mighty revelation/ una you are called, oldest of plants.
> Stephen Pollington, Leechcraft: *Early English Charms Plantlore and Healing*

You can make a herb oil from your favourite herb (or herbs) by adding some plant matter into the oil and leaving it on a warm, sunny shelf for a few days; afterwards, strain it so that just the infused oil is left. You may find your new runes will need several applications to let them fully absorb the oil.

When you have blooded and dressed your runes you will need to find or make a bag for them. The bag can be made of leather or cloth and you may like to decorate it or, if you prefer, leave it plain. Once the runes have their own bag you can continue with the magical charging. This process is really down to traditions on consecration: you may wish to expose your runes to the light of the full moon and/or you may wish to expose them to the midday sun. You may wish to sprinkle them with sea water or water from a natural spring. All of these things add to the connection between you, your runes and Wyrd. One of the things I did was to hang my runes in an ash tree that I often keep company with: for me this created a connection with Woden and the World Tree.

Connecting with your runes

Once you have connected your runes with nature it is time to connect your runes to you. You can do this by putting them under your pillow at night and by carrying them with you next to your skin. Most importantly, you should connect with them by handling them, picking the up one by one and looking at them, feeling them and thinking about their individual meanings. You should handle one rune a day: carry it with you, become familiar with its shape and feel, and make sure you note in your journal any connections that you find during the day, or any that you remember from your dreams, and how they relate to this rune. Most importantly, do what comes naturally. You could ask the runes what they think you should do.

How to work with your runes

Looking for historical evidence on the different magical uses of runes in England is not so easy, but there is a good chance that divination continued from the Germanic example that Tacitus gives us. The most famous English example, often given as proof of the magical use of runes, comes from the Venerable Bede's *Ecclesiastical History*, iv.20. It's a story about a young man named Imma, who was taken prisoner after a battle between the Northumbrians and Mercians and whose captors could not bind him without the ties falling off. Bede puts this down to Imma's brother being an abbot who, thinking Imma dead, prayed for him at each mass. However, within the story a section is found where Imma's captors ask if he has loosening runes on his person. In Old English the word 'rune' means a spell, charm or secret: it was not associated with the runes as we know them today until after the Vikings came to stay, and Imma's story was written before then, in 649 CE. What Imma's story does show us is that whatever script the charm was written in, a loosening charm was known and this is evidence that magical practice of this kind existed in England.

Although nothing much can be found in Old English manuscripts, we can turn to Old Norse examples. *The Poetic Edda* of Iceland seems to contain the richest source of information concerning runic magic. In the famous section known as the *Hávamál* (Odin's tale of the runes), verses 139 to 165 tell of how he first found the runes and of the rune charms he learned. Verse 150 shows that there are runes for loosening bonds.

> *150. A fourth I know, | if men shall fasten*
> *Bonds on my bended legs;*
> *So great is the charm | that forth I may go,*
> *The fetters spring from my feet,*
> *Broken the bonds from my hands.*
> Henry Adams Bellows'(1885-1939) translation for the American-Scandinavian Foundation.

The following are verses 5-19 of the *Sigrdrífumál* which tells of some of the uses of runes:

> *5. "Beer I bring thee, | tree of battle,*
> *Mingled of strength | and mighty fame;*
> *Charms it holds | and healing signs,*
> *Spells full good, | and gladness-runes."*

6. Winning-runes learn, | if thou longest to win,
And the runes on thy sword-hilt write;
Some on the furrow, | and some on the flat,
And twice shalt thou call on Tyr.

7. Ale-runes learn, | that with lies the wife
Of another betray not thy trust;
On the horn thou shalt write, | and the backs of thy hands,
And Need shalt mark on thy nails.
Thou shalt bless the draught, | and danger escape,
And cast a leek in the cup;
(For so I know | thou never shalt see
Thy mead with evil mixed.)

8. Birth-runes learn, | if help thou wilt lend,
The babe from the mother to bring;
On thy palms shalt write them, | and round thy joints,
And ask the fates to aid.

9. Wave-runes learn, | if well thou wouldst shelter
The sail-steeds out on the sea;
On the stem shalt thou write, | and the steering blade,
And burn them into the oars;
Though high be the breakers, | and black the waves,
Thou shalt safe the harbour seek.

10. Branch-runes learn, | if a healer wouldst be,
And cure for wounds wouldst work;
On the bark shalt thou write, | and on trees that be
With boughs to the eastward bent.

11. Speech-runes learn, | that none may seek
To answer harm with hate;
Well he winds | and weaves them all,
And sets them side by side,
At the judgment-place, | when justice there
The folk shall fairly win.

12. Thought-runes learn, | if all shall think
Thou art keenest minded of men.

Making and working with runes

13. Them Hropt arranged, | and them he wrote,
And them in thought he made,
Out of the draught | that down had dropped
From the head of Heithdraupnir,
And the horn of Hoddrofnir.

14. On the mountain he stood | with Brimir's sword,
On his head the helm he bore;
Then first the head | of Mim spoke forth,
And words of truth it told.

15. He bade write on the shield | before the shining goddess,
On Arvak's ear, | and on Alsvith's hoof,
On the wheel of the car | of Hrungnir's killer,
On Sleipnir's teeth, | and the straps of the sledge.

16. On the paws of the bear, | and on Bragi's tongue,
On the wolf's claws bared, | and the eagle's beak,
On bloody wings, | and bridge's end,
On freeing hands | and helping foot-prints.

17. On glass and on gold, | and on goodly charms,
In wine and in beer, | and on well-loved seats,
On Gungnir's point, | and on Grani's breast,
On the nails of Norns, | and the night-owl's beak.

18. Shaved off were the runes | that of old were written,
And mixed with the holy mead,
And sent on ways so wide;
So the gods had them, | so the elves got them,
And some for the Wanes so wise,
And some for mortal men.

19. Beech-runes are there, | birth-runes are there,
And all the runes of ale,
And the magic runes of might;
Who knows them rightly | and reads them true,
Has them himself to help;
Ever they aid,
Till the gods are gone.

Finally a couple more verses from the *Hávamál'* where Odin mentions runes of divination and necromancy.

> *79. Certain is that | which is sought from runes,*
> *That the gods so great have made,*
> *And the Master-Poet painted;*
>
> *. . . . .*
> *. . . . . of the race of gods:*
> *Silence is safest and best.*
>
> *158. A twelfth I know, | if high on a tree*
> *I see a hanged man swing;*
> *So do I write | and colour the runes*
> *That forth he fares,*
> *And to me talks.*
> Henry Adams Bellows'(1885-1939) translation for the American-Scandinavian Foundation.

'Verse 79' has been corrupted but it does appear to indicate divination and 'verse 158' famously describes Odin talking to the dead.

Egil's Saga, an Icelandic saga on the life of Egil Skallagrímsson -a farmer, Viking warrior and skald (poet) - is also a rich source runic magic especially the part where Egil discovers and destroys a poisoned drink by carving runes on the drinking horn and then painting them with his blood. The painting of runes with blood appears in other early Norse literature, but there is controversy here with some scholars believing this aspect is invented to make the stories more colourful.

If you have read this book from the beginning then you should be well prepared to start your rune-working journey. If you have kept your journal then you will find your entries of great help. If you haven't kept a journal then I suggest you start one now because, although you can flip back and forth through this book, your own experience is the key to becoming a rune master.

Part 5

Divination

Divination

What is meant by divination

If you have skipped to this chapter, don't worry: simple divination practice can help you discover more about your runes in a practical way.

Divination with runes won't tell you what will happen in the future but it will let you know the possibilities: this is because Wyrd is not set in stone, but a journey of possibilities and choices. These possibilities come to light through asking questions and looking at the responses. Quite often runes can be very blunt in their response so even yes/no questions can be answered, provided the question is clear. When you first begin it is a good idea to take no notice of which way the runes appear. Considering inverted runes at this point can really complicate matters and to be honest many people do not consider them at all.

Before using your runes

Remember that before you work with your runes you should always greet them and ask them for their help. Remember that these runes are entities in their own right and you are in a relationship with them. If you have any specific spiritual guides or gods that you work with, then you should acknowledge them too.

Reading for yourself

Many people advise that you should never read for yourself because you may only see what you want to see. This may be true but it is good practice to read for yourself, especially while learning. This practice helps engender the discipline to read what is there, warts and all. Without being honest with yourself, you can't read the runes effectively.

Rune of the day

This is the best way to start divining with runes. Sleeping with your runes under your pillow and keeping them close to you while you are learning acts as a reminder for this practice.

When you wake up in the morning, say good morning to your runes and ask them what your day holds for you. Put your hand in the bag and let your senses pick one rune; take it out and look at the rune you have chosen – you can even say hello. You should keep the rune close to you through the day, perhaps in a small bag round your neck or pinned onto your clothing. Don't forget that your runes are your magical ally. Write down your immediate thoughts before you check the meaning in your journal or in this book. These first thoughts may surprise you: they may not even match your knowledge of this rune, they may seem totally unconnected, but they are most important because these thoughts are connected to your intuition.

After you have noted this, you can add your most up-to-date meaning for this rune – I say 'most up-to-date' because you should expect the meaning to change slightly as your relationship grows. Then go out and live your day.

During the day you may spot things you immediately recognise as related to this rune: note these. You may not notice anything at all – don't worry, it doesn't matter.

At the end of the day before you sleep you should gaze on your rune, think about the day you have had and note any connections you found. Finally, say thank you to your rune for its help and guidance and put it back with the others.

When you feel ready or feel the need you can start to ask questions of your rune of the day. You can work in the way described above to build confidence if you wish, or you can ask your question and read the answer you are given, thank the rune and then put it away. Again, it is good to write about this in your rune of the day and/or study journal; these journals are a physical store of your experience and rune knowledge, and it also acts as an historical record of your journey that can be looked at in years to come.

Reading for others

When you feel confident, feel free to start reading for others. This is where your honesty, integrity and credibility are most important. Honesty can be difficult because we do not want to cause distress, but if you have learned to be honest with yourself then this experience will really help; it will also enable you to understand and express the subtleties of the runic responses. Your integrity will show in your truthfulness, reliability and honour; always keep your promises, never gossip, and definitely never make things up just because you aren't connecting on a particular day. By following these basic tenets your credibility will shine through.

Divination

If you have followed the guide on reading for yourself, you should also have built up confidence in your own intuition. This is possibly the most difficult thing to express to your client because your thoughts and feelings may not make any sense to you at all. To start with, you can say things like, 'This doesn't make any sense to me but I am feeling that ...', 'What do you think?' or 'This might not mean anything to you but ...'. It is amazing how often something that seems totally off the wall actually has relevance.

Past, present, future

There are many reading patterns and types you can use, but it is probably best to start with the most simple. Three runes: the first to give a background to the question, the second to see what is happening now or how the present is affected, and the third to give an idea of the possible outcome. Always make sure the client has asked a question and never get into a situation where the client stays silent and expects you to give an outcome without clues: you are not a fortune teller. It is guidance that you are offering.

Sit calmly with your client and ask them what they would like guidance on. You need to know this because your client may not be able phrase the question or questions properly when asking the runes. When the question to ask has been decided on, you can continue.

Greet your runes and guides (silently if you wish) and tell them that you need their support to help your client. It is best to create a ritual that you can employ for requesting help, for example: close your eyes, whisper your request, put your hands in the bag and caress your runes. It is important that your client sees you treat your runes with respect and reverence.

When this has been done you can pass the runes to your client and get them to think of their question while choosing three runes, one at a time. These runes should be laid on your cloth, top to bottom or right to left, in a straight line or a curved one, the choice is yours.

Look at the runes and see what your intuition says about them, and then leave that thought until a bit later. Next, talk to your client about the question and the first rune that they have picked: this is indicating the background. Then look at and discuss what is going on at the moment, and follow this up with what is possible in the future. Make sure you use the language of possibility here; the client may be happy with the possibility you are presenting, but, if this is not the case, you can look at ways of influencing change. It is in discussion that you can employ your first thoughts and use them where necessary. The client's ideas on the background to the situation are clouded by their own wants and needs, but your intuition may be telling you otherwise and it could be something the client needs to reflect on.

The past, present, future spread can be expanded to three for each area, nine in total; this will give you more information for an expanded reading. Maybe one part of a reading is not as clear as it could be or there are further questions arising – in either case you could get the client to choose another rune. This is totally up to your instincts around the situation.

For other reading spreads the world is your oyster: you can use tarot spreads such as the Celtic cross, or look up some other runes spreads. You can of course throw the chosen runes onto a marked cloth and see where they land. With more experience you may even create your own reading method.

After the reading

When you have finished your reading you should thank your runes and your guides for their help, you can do this in the same manner as you greeted them. Sometimes after a reading you may feel that your runes need a bit of loving care: remember, if it is rough on you, it is rough on them too. At these moments it is a good idea to dress them again with oil and while you are doing this sing to them gently, concentrating on one at a time, and reconnect. For singing to your runes, take a look at the section on Galdor.

Rune cloth

It is a good idea to use a rune cloth to protect your charged runes from unclean surfaces. Tacitus talks about the Germanic peoples using a white cloth; he does not describe any markings on that cloth and to be honest a plain cloth is all you need. Depending on how you develop your way of reading, you may decide on a more detailed cloth that is marked out into specific areas. These areas can be based on the twelve astrological houses, or concentric circles defining past, present and future. I recommend starting with a plain cloth, but you should always go with what feels best for you.

Part 6

Magical uses

Amulets and talismans

Amulets and Talismans are found the world over and are evident in most spiritualities and religions: they are the 'lucky charms' we all love. Many of us think of them as the same thing, and in fact some dictionaries describe them in the same way, but to a great number of those who practice magic there is a difference, and in order to use them magically it is important to know this difference.

> **Amulet** – used to ward off evil spirits, illness and other negative energies. People have used amulets for centuries: things such as garlic, coal, lucky coins, horseshoes, crucifixes and runes are worn, carried or used in the home for protection. Although they can be specifically created, they are often made from natural found objects. The word 'amulet' comes from the Latin word *amuletum*.
>
> **Talisman** – used to give positive energy to people and to enhance strength, also to help draw positive energies towards a person. A talisman is a lucky charm, and is usually made for a specific purpose. The word 'talisman' comes from the Byzantine Greek word *telesma*.

Both can be made with or without using runes; we will concentrate on the use of runes, but feel free to use other scripts.

Magical formulae
There are a few historic runic combinations that can be considered magical formulae. They confuse literary scholars who have tried to translate them as words: although some appear to be words, it is unlikely in all cases.

ALU

This is probably the most famous magical word and is often thought to mean 'ale', due to its association with drinking horns, as it has been found on them and is believed to protect the horn and, in turn, the user of the horn, from poisoning. It has also been found on many other items not associated with ale, so it is highly possible that ALU is not actually a word.

ᚠᚢᚦᚨᚱᚲᚺᚹᚾᛁᛏᛂᛁᚣᛇᛏᛒᛗᛉᚻᛚᛝᛟᚳᛠ

An English runic example of FUTHORC from the Thames Scramasax

The Futhark or Futhorc is often carved in full; no one really knows the reason for this, but it is likely to have a magical context. Finds that show the Futhark carved in its full form have enabled scholars to translate runes. The oldest of these is the Kylver Stone, which is believed to be a grave top and was found with the runes facing inward.

ᛚᚨᚢᚲᚨᛉ

LAUKAZ

This is the Germanic word for leek and as a magical word it appears to be associated with fertility. It is often found together with *lin*, the Germanic word for linen or flax. Both of these words are connected with fertility and preservation. The idea behind the use of LAUKAZ may come from an earlier time, attested by the use of the leek by the Welsh. When more than one culture holds a similar belief it often suggests a common usage prior to separation.

Bind runes and mirror runes

Bind runes and mirror runes are often used in rune magic today and can be found in the old rune carvings. Bind runes are usually two or more runes carved together making them one, and mirror runes are usually a single rune mirrored and joined on its axis.

ᚻᚢ

ALU as a bind rune

Literary scholars tend to believe that bind runes are created due to lack of space on the object being carved but, since spells tended to be written on surfaces that were also small and often not designed to last, then it is very possible that runes were bound together for magical purposes.

Magical Uses

Modern-day bind runes

Mirror runes are literally written as they would be seen held against a mirror, reflected from the point they touch. As you can see below, this actually disguises the runes so they can't be read easily.

ALU as a mirror rune

Both bind runes and mirror runes are excellent for amulets and talismans.

The following are two examples of Icelandic amulets or talismans; they are from a later period, but give us a good idea of what can be created with some imagination

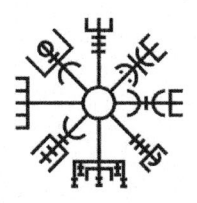

Vegvísir is used so that you never lose your way in storms and bad weather, even if you don't know the way in the first place.

Ægishjálmur is known as the Helm of Awe and traditionally it was believed to have been painted or carved onto the foreheads of warriors to strike fear into their enemies. It may also have been painted on shields.

How to make an amulet or talisman

Before you start do your research, ask yourself why you are making an amulet or talisman; you need to know the whole story, so ask questions and listen carefully. It may be that the need for an amulet or talisman was discovered during a divination or, if not, it may be that divination will help you find the right runes to use. You should ask yourself and even your client:

- What is the reason for this charm?
- Do you want one for the client to keep close or for it to be given to nature?

Choose your runes. If you are making a bind rune then find three runes, or two if you can't identify a third that will help the situation. These runes can be put together to create one shape; it may take several goes at putting the runes in different places within the shape before you find the one that feels right. It is a good idea for the runes not to be individually recognisable. You may decide on mirror runes, where you can choose one or more runes to help.

Choose your medium. If you are handing the amulet or talisman to the client to wear, then you need to create something like a small pendant, which could be made of leather, cloth, or wood; or perhaps it might be something that they can carry in a small pouch or in their purse - the choices are only limited by your imagination. Whatever you decide, you will need to mark the runes you have chosen onto it.

While you are marking the amulet or talisman you should sing or intone the runes as you mark them, and as soon as you have finished you should put it out of sight. Once created and charged with Galdor, the amulet or talisman becomes an entity in its own right and neither you nor your client should be looking at the runes. It would be like looking at someone you have met and seeing their head, legs, arms and torso but not the whole person. One of the main reasons for using bind runes and mirror runes in magic is that they hide the individual runes.

Another way to make an amulet or talisman is to mark the runes on paper, charge them then burn the paper and include the ash within it. You may come up with other ingenious methods of creating amulets and talismans for clients, and you can even create them as presents for loved ones when they need a little extra help or luck.

When you pass these 'charms' on to someone you should always advise that they are to help, not solve, for example: 'Here is a little something to help you with your interview, but remember it can't help you if you don't help yourself.' Please don't let anyone think that these work on

Magical Uses

their own; they can only influence a situation, not change it, as we all have the free will to ignore common sense. The use of runes without giving advice does happen and this usually relies on the rune master knowing how the recipient will behave. If someone has a weak spot, this has often been exploited – and not in a good way – so, in order to avoid this, openness and honesty are the best policy.

Part 7

Galdor

What is Galdor?

Galdor, sometimes spelled *gealdor*, is an Old English word based on the word *galan* (sing, chant), and is used specifically in reference to an incantation and enchantment. Galdor is magic that is intoned, chanted or sung and this is most often as part of a charm.

It is likely that the early English put trust in the effect of the voice and this is certainly true today: we sing our children to sleep, and we talk about people with hypnotic voices. The early English had enchanters and they practised *galdor-cræftiga*, the enchanter's craft was Galdor. Today we tend to think of this magic in a supernatural context, but to the early English living in a more animistic society it was natural, not supernatural. The right words sung the right way with the right gestures could influence and bend the path of the web towards a different outcome in Wyrd. In essence, the enchanter would sing to persuade herbs to help him/her cure illness and sing to persuade the spirit of an illness to leave.

Charms

We are lucky to have at our disposal a number of medical herbals written in Old English that have been translated and studied by many scholars over the years. These medical herbals, especially *The Lacnunga*, contain charms which specify the ingredients, words and actions that are to be used.

Unfortunately they give no clue as to how they were sung or intoned, so it is for us to imagine and put into practice. Although these Old English charms and recipes do not contain runes, it is possible that there were some including them that have been lost. One charm in particular, the 'Charm for Unfruitful Land', is very complex and partly involves taking four pieces of turf from around the land into the church for blessing. When they are returned to the land they need to have small wooden crosses, made from aspen wood and marked with saints' names, placed beneath them. It is so easy to rethink this part of the charm by using runes intoned and marked on aspen staves for the protection and blessing of the land. It is very likely that this charm was taken on by the Church because the people who worked the land would have been using a pre-Christian version and would not have wanted to lose something that worked. As such, the Church would want to be involved and so needed it to be updated into Christian belief.

Runes

We have already discussed runes and their connection with Wyrd; we have also discussed making runes and developing a relationship with them as beings in their own right. However, runes do not exist solely in written format – they also exist in sound form. Each rune shape represents a sound and each has a name. Runes are sound-energy beings: they exist in the ether and when chanted or sung they travel distances, great or small, carrying your intent. It is not quite as simple as this; it requires knowledge and practice but is well worth the effort.

From the meanings below we can see that this involves singing in some form, but please don't let it worry you as the singing involved is not judged. The perfect note to sing here is one that comes naturally to you and not one a singing teacher would expect. Everyone has their own tone and pitch and I am sure that the runes have been called in every tone and pitch conceivable. Let's consider the definition of Galdor as the process of intoning, chanting or singing:

> Intone – *say or recite with little rise and fall in the pitch of the voice.*
>
> Chant – *say or shout repeatedly in a sing-song tone.*
>
> Sing – *make musical sounds with the voice, especially words with a set tune.*
> *Or make a high-pitched whistling or buzzing sound.*

The runes can be sung on one note, any note that feels right to you, or a note which changes very slightly, perhaps a semi-tone. You may choose to start on one note and then add others. You can also use other sounds such as the ones suggested above – buzzing or whistling or hissing – and this entirely depends on what the magic is for. All you need to do is find your voice.

Finding your voice

Your voice is one of the most important tools you possess, but also for many of us our singing voice is one of the things we are most shy of using. Don't panic though, the voice you need here is the one that sings along in the car or in the bath. We do not need perfection; we need to feel the sound and send it out.

Singing vowels

The first aspect to practise for singing or intoning runes is singing the vowels: 'A', 'E', 'I', 'O', 'U', plus 'AE' and 'Y'. They seem to naturally have a scale of their own starting with 'I' as the top note then 'E', 'A', 'O', 'U'. Vowels should be sung as long notes and the best way to start is to take a deep breath and sing the note on an out breath for as long as the out breath takes.

> 'I' - is sung 'ee'; this is a high note and it doesn't matter which high note you choose. While you sing this note think of singing in the area behind your third eye.
> 'Y' - is sung like an 'ee' with 'oo' lips; if you start by singing 'ee' then change your lip shape to an 'oo', and you will find that the note naturally sounds slightly lower.
> 'E' - is sung like 'eh' in egg, but longer; this note should be lower than the 'I' and you should think about your throat at your Adam's apple area.
> 'Æ' - is sung 'aa' like the 'a' in apple, but longer; you should think of the sound resonating halfway between the throat and the heart.
> 'A' - is sung 'ah', like the 'a' in bath said with a posh accent. Once again, it's a lower note than 'E'; this time think of the sound being in the middle of your chest, in the heart area.
> 'O' - is sung like o in orange, remembering to keep the note long and slightly lower than A. You should be thinking of the area around the solar plexus, just below the ribcage centre-front.
> 'U' - is sung like 'oo', as in who without the 'wh'. This is the lowest note and you should think of the area just above the pubic bone.

Practice

The best way to practice singing the vowels is to find a quiet place, perhaps in the countryside, where there are not many people. This will help you to let go and sing loud, and not worry that you are going to embarrass yourself. You can also sneak into the bathroom; close the windows and door, and let rip. Standing up makes it easier. To start, take some slow, deep breaths right to the bottom of your lungs. After a few breaths you can find a high note and start with 'I' on the next breath out; then breathe in again, and breathe out to 'E'; then breathe in and sing next note down on the out breath, and so on. If it is confusing, don't worry about singing the 'Æ' or 'Y' when you first start; thinking about two extra vowels may put you off the singing. Add them when you are comfortable or remember them.

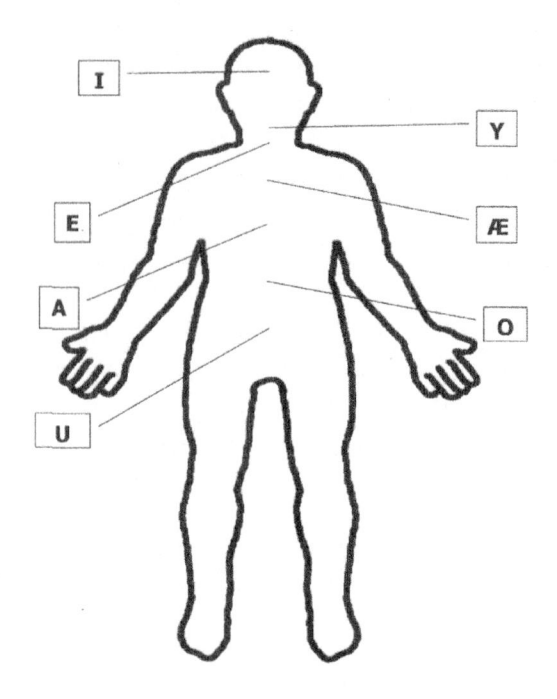

Chart showing the areas of expression when singing the vowels

- Don't worry if you feel you need to take a break; it can be difficult to start with, and taking slow, deep breaths can also make you feel a little dizzy because we don't often breathe this way. You will get used to it.

- Don't worry if you find you are starting on a different high each time, even for the same letter, this is totally natural and should be expected.

- Don't be afraid to use your arms and change your stance while singing – do what comes naturally.

When you have practised this a few times, you can have a go at starting from 'U' and going up. Practice is very important and you will start to find it very meditative.

Singing the Runes into being

So you are now ready to practice singing some of the rune names. As with all words the rune names have vowels and it is these you should concentrate on to start with. Remember that sometimes it feels natural to have the high notes higher or lower than at other times, but once you find the note for your starting vowel try and make sure that the others are in relation to it. Old English is a phonetic language which means that all of the letters are pronounced; most consonants are the same as modern English but the following are different.

> 'C' is pronounced 'ch' as in church when next to a front vowel sound like 'I' or 'E' it is also pronounced this way when doubled 'CC' in the middle of a word.
> 'C' is pronounced 'k' when next to a back vowel like 'A', 'O' or 'U'.
> 'G' is pronounced like the 'y' in yellow when used before 'E' or 'I'.
> 'G' is pronounced like the 'g' in gold when used before 'A', 'O' or 'U'.
> 'G' is pronounced with a soft 'g' almost like the 'ch' in loch, but with a very slight vocal growling sound. Sometimes it falls silent at the end of a word, especially where it becomes obvious that the language developed in this way - for example, *dæg* is pronounced 'day' and *mæg* is pronounced 'may'.
> 'H' is pronounced as an out breath, so *hlafod* is pronounced with an aspirated 'L' in the same way as 'LL' in Welsh. You may find that at the end of some words 'H' sounds like a soft 'ch' as in loch.
> 'SC' is 'sh' as in ship.
> 'F' is pronounced as it is in modern English at the beginning of a word, but when used in the middle of the word it sounds like a 'V'.
> 'R' is trilled, but this is not so easy for singing. It is better to position your tongue as if to trill, but without actually trilling.

When you sing runes you will be connecting with the runes that already exist as sound beings within the Web of Wyrd, and for this reason it is a good idea to speak your intention to practise and to request their patience. Sound beings are often contacted unknowingly and have learned to ignore noise, but when they are contacted directly they can be helpful: always treat them with respect.

Becoming more experimental

When you look back at the definitions you will see that singing included high notes and buzzing; this means it can include hissing, growling and other animal noises. With this idea in mind take another look at the rune meanings and you might find that some can be enhanced by using these vocal methods, for example: Ur is an Aurochs and you can imagine a low, rumbling, growling sound with the 'U'.

If you are creating an amulet or talisman, or using runes for other Galdor magic, then you should always follow your intuition on how the Galdor should be sung. There will be occasions, for instance if you are making a wedding blessing, when you feel your voice should be light and happy in which case go with your intuition.

Appendix

Rune table

Rune	Letter	Basic divination meanings and ideas
ᚠ Feoh Wealth	f	Money, Generosity | Comfort | Sharing money or skills | Things that can be sold to raise money | Skills you have that can be exchanged for money
ᚢ Ūr Aurochs	u	Strength, bodily or mental | Proud and Brave | Initiation | Rite of Passage | Independent | Courageous | Worthy of joining the club | Adulthood
ᚦ Thorn Thurs	þ, ð, th	Sharp | Causing pain and discomfort | Menstrual pain, women's problems, heavy blood loss, peri-menopausal symptoms | Being attacked | Giant | Defence, of friends, family, property
ᚩ Ōs God Woden	o	Wisdom | Prophetic speech | Common sense | Source of comfort through understanding and insight | Woden as the wise one | Healing | Frenzy | Confidence
ᚱ Rād Riding	r	Travel, road, pathway | Mode of transport, car, motorbike etc | Furniture/seating of the transport and in the home Pride of ownership | Boasting

Rune	Letter	Basic divination meanings and ideas
ᚳ Cēn Torch	c	Bright light | Clarity | Knowledge | Information gained through discussion with others | Keen, brave, bold | Conceive, create
ᚷ Gyfu Gift	g	Giving and receiving | Conditional vs. unconditional | Gratitude | Relationship | Responsibility | Honour and reputation
ᚹ Wen Happiness	w	Joy, bliss | Recognition and understanding of a happy state | Lack of poverty | Ability to rise out of the depths | People who support you | Friends and family you can trust
ᚻ Hægl Hail	h	Something temptingly beautiful that disappears | Sudden devastation | A promise that turns to nothing | Look beneath the surface | Beware a con
ᚾ Nȳd Need	n	Necessity, obligation, service | The gut feeling of need or want | Recognised early it can be lessened or understood | A shaper of Wyrd
ᛁ Īs Ice	i	Frozen, extreme cold | Slippery and dangerous | Difficult to negotiate | Beauty or temptation, best viewed from a place of safety | Slow moving | Appears stuck

The English Runes

Rune	Letter	Basic divination meanings and ideas
Gēr Harvest	j	Year, end of the year | A blessing or good outcome | Planning for the next season/year | Decisions to be made, may be difficult
Ēoh Yew	eo	A fire keeper, Slow burning |Unsmooth and ancient | Everlasting |Connection to ancestors | Important part of your homeland or place you love
Peorð Gaming	p	Companionship |Pleasure and laughter | A Gamble | Life on the edge | Sudden change | A doorway to another realm | Liminal space
Eolhx Elk	x	Independent, Protective, Adaptable | Will fight if cornered | Wounds | Divine Twins | Grove, Sanctuary |Cross dressing | Shape changing | Gender dysphoria or fluidity
Sigel Sun	s	Navigation | Guidance during daylight | Safety | Overseas travel | Positive signs and indications
Tīr Tiw, a God	t	A sign that holds true | Guidance after dark | The pole star |A God of War and Judgement | Luck in battle | A connection with ancestors | The Green man

Rune	Letter	Basic divination meanings and ideas
ᛒ Beorc Birch	b	Beginning , Pioneering, Adaptable, Nurturing | Spring | Fire | Tall and beautiful |Family connections | Communications, through roots and as paper |Fire starter, water holder, container
ᛖ Eh Horse	e	Sovereignty | Freedom |Restless spirit | Help in carrying loads, people, goods, burdens
ᛗ Man Mankind	m	Friendship | Love | Relationship | Security of community | Fallibility | Can only be relied upon in the short term
ᛚ Lagu Water	l	Large body of water | Emotions | Rules | Law | If you don't follow the rules then you will come unstuck | Control of emotions and your destiny
ᛝ Ing A God, Frea	ŋ	Fertility and Family ties | A fertile field | Blessings of the Earth Mother | A journey Eastward | Pilgrimage | Peace | Banishing of weapons
ᛟ Ēðel Homeland	œ	Inheritance | Family land |Tribal land | The place you feel most at home | Place you yearn for | Spirits of your place of connection

The English Runes

Rune	Letter	Basic divination meanings and ideas
ᛞ Dæg Day	d	Daylight | A working day | Productive time | See things clearly | Shines light in the dark places| Chases the monsters away
ᚪ Āc Oak	a	Strength | Endurance | A national symbol | Free foods for animals | Forests | Autumn | Acorns | Boats | A world tree | Thunor or Thor
ᚫ Æsc Ash	œ	World Tree Yggdrasil | Strong, tall, straight | Protective against force | Fuel for warmth, burns green | A primal being | Creation story ancestor
ᛇ ȳr Yew bow	y	Skill | The very best equipment | Attractive accessory | Fighting force | Surprise attack | Overwhelming
ᛡ Īar Beaver	ia, io	Home building | Place of safety | Comfortable abode | Good food | Hard work, with results | Determination
ᛠ Ēar Grave	ea	Death | All things must end | Sacrifice | John Barley Corn | An ear of corn | The cycle of life | End of one life cycle

Bibliography

Bosworth-Toller Anglo-Saxon dictionary www.bosworthtoller.com

This is an online edition of *An Anglo-Saxon Dictionary*, or a dictionary of "Old English". The dictionary records the state of the English language as it was used between ca. 700-1100 AD by the Anglo-Saxon inhabitants of the British Isles. *Based on the manuscript collections of the late Joseph Bosworth* (the so called Main Volume, first edition 1898) and its *Supplement* (first edition 1921), edited by **Joseph Bosworth** and **T. Northcote Toller**, today the largest complete dictionary of Old English. Alistair Campbell's "enlarged addenda and corrigenda" from 1972 are not public domain and are therefore not part of the online dictionary. http://bosworth.ff.cuni.cz/

Referenced books:

Billington, Penny — *The Wisdom of Birch Oak and Yew* (Llewellyn Publications, 2015)

Gooley, Tristan — *The Natural Navigator* (Virgin Books, 2010)

Kemble, John M. — *Anglo-Saxon Runes* (Anglo-Saxon Books, 1991

Macfarlane, Robert — *The Old Ways A Journey on Foot* (The Penguin Group, 2012)

Pollington, Stephen — *Rudiments of Runelore* (Anglo-Saxon Books, 1995)

Runes: Literacy in the Germanic Iron Age (Anglo-Saxon Books, 2016)

The Elder Gods: The Otherworld of Early England (Anglo-Saxon Books, 2011)

Leechcraft: Early English Charms Plantlore and Healing (Anglo-Saxon Books, 2000)

Referenced listening:

The Ballad of John Barleycorn from *The Hills They Are Hollow* (July 2003) www.paganmusic.co.uk

Referenced Website:

Anglo-Saxon Aloud produced by Michael D. C. Drout, Prentice Professor of English at Wheaton College, Norton, MA. Search for: anglo saxon aloud michael drout

Suggested reading:

Bates, Brian	*The Way of Wyrd* (Hay House UK, 2004)
	The Real Middle Earth: Magic and Mystery in the Dark Ages (Sedgwick & Jackson, 2002)
Lacey, R Danziger, D.	THE YEAR 1000: What life was like at the turn of the First Millennium (Little Brown and Company, 1999)
Page, R.I. 1973)	An Introduction to the English Runes (Boydell Press,
	Runes: Reading the Past (The British Museum Press, 1987)

Suggested Websites:

www.tha-engliscan-gesithas.org.uk A society for all those interested in the history and culture of Anglo-Saxon England, including the language and literature, archaeology, anthropology, architecture, art, religion, mythology, folklore and material culture.

Companion Journals:

Two journals are available through Amazon:

The English Runes: *Study Journal*
The English Runes: *Rune of the Day Journal*

Printed in Great Britain
by Amazon